What Rea

Glory! THE LEGACY OF ONE ORDINARY WOMAN
AND HER EXTRAORDINARY GOD

At the beginning of Jesus' ministry, some of John's disciples ran after Jesus who was on His way to another place. When they asked Him where He was staying, He said, "Come…and you will see." They followed Him, but not to a house; rather, into a Kingdom realm. Dabney Mann could have easily been one of these disciples. In a way, she was—and is. During her lifetime, Dabney has had many amazing front-row seats in Jesus' Kingdom as she found Him and followed Him around the globe, joining Him in His epic work of redemption.

Glory! is a rich and inspirational account of one woman's pursuit of Jesus, His love, His truth, and the power to save, heal and deliver by the Spirit. Dabney has had passport-filling, remarkable ministry journeys to many nations of the world, as well as powerful encounters in the streets, churches and synagogues of Middle Tennessee. These experiences have resulted in innumerable changed lives—including her own and those of the young people, women, and men she has ministered with and to. I should know, because I am one of them, having traveled with her husband Doug and Dabney. In her moving memoir, Jesus invites each of *us*, "Come…and you will see!" If you accept His invitation, be prepared for a renewed walk with Him as you devour the pages of this book.

—MICK ANTANAITIS
World Outreach. Pastor Emeritus, Belmont Church

If I were to attempt to sum up the content of this book, *Glory!*, I might try something like this: "The Impact of a Life Extraordinarily Well Lived." Since I have known Dabney Mann for many years as an intercessor, missionary, godly wife, mother, grandmother, role model and mentor to many and as a personal friend, I thought I had surely heard about all of her exploits in Christ. But hidden away in these pages are jewels to be mined by the careful reader. For like the Proverbs 31 woman, "In her is found hidden treasures beyond the knowledge of man." O, what a Legacy, indeed!

—Dr. James W. Goll
Founder, God Encounters Ministries, GOLL Ideation LLC

Throughout history, women have been used by God. Many women in the Bible were given opportunities to be history-makers. Esther risked her life and saved a nation by her obedience. Deborah ruled as a righteous judge. Jael made sure that the wicked king would rule no more. Mary said yes to carrying the Savior of the world, even though it cost her much. Women were the first at the tomb of our resurrected Lord. Their desperation, obedience and their yes changed history. They were willing to risk everything. Dabney Mann is to be listed alongside these brave, courageous women who said yes!
Following God's call isn't about qualifications. It isn't about education or heritage. Following the Lord is about pursuing Him and saying yes. Our steps of obedience open the doors, and He creates adventures we never dreamed possible.

It has been my joy to know Dabney for over 25 years and to join her on several of her journeys. Not only has she said yes to God for herself, but she has truly "made disciples" along the way as women, young and old, follow her yes. You will enjoy reading about this ordinary woman whom God has used to do extraordinary things. Along the way, you may be challenged to say, "Yes, Lord, whatever you want me to do, I will do it!" If so, get ready for an adventure!

—Cindi Whitman
Executive Director, Restoring the Foundations

To the casual observer, Dabney Mann may appear to be "an ordinary woman." Sorry, but let me assure you—there is nothing ordinary about her! Following the exploits to which she has given herself so generously, the world has drastically changed. What hasn't changed is Dabney's continual passion for the Lord, her spiritual hunger, and her prompt obedience when He calls. Let the words of this book ignite a fire and passion within you to step into your own glorious adventures with Him.

—MICKEY ROBINSON, AUTHOR, SPEAKER, FRIEND
Founder, Prophetic Destiny International

Dabney Mann has led a life worthy of any of the heroines of the faith we have read about—Deborah, Ruth, Lottie Moon, to mention a few. She has the unique ability and wisdom to capture a given situation with a word picture or phrase that impacts the reader to the core and brings them to the foot of the Cross with a choice to be made: Will I trust Jesus with my all? And she does it with the simplest, yet most profound wit and candor that only those who truly know Him could accomplish. This book will fill you with faith, help set you free from any hindrance, and impart a greater passion for Him.

Dabney, my beloved friend, like your forebear Sir James, with fearless courage, YOU carry the King of kings' heart to all you meet. Thank you for "washing the feet" of His children with your words and actions. May we all go and do likewise.

—KIM DRIVER
Director, Heartland National Prayer Alliance

Glory!

THE LEGACY OF ONE ORDINARY
WOMAN AND HER EXTRAORDINARY GOD

Glory!

DABNEY MANN

With Anne Severance

"Ask of Me, and I will give you the nations."
—*Psalm 2:8*

—

"For the earth will be filled with the knowledge
of the glory of the LORD, as the waters cover the sea."
—*Habakkuk 2:14*

CONTENTS

FOREWORD

I have just finished reading Dabney Mann's book and I am stunned.

Not that I was unaware of this "ordinary woman and her extraordinary God."

Not that I was unaware of some of the remarkable journeys and amazing testimonies this ordinary woman had as she traveled the world, often making forays into enemy territory in order to bring Holy Spirit fullness and light into the world's deepest despair.

Not that I was unaware of the impact that this ordinary woman had here at home as she, like Deborah so long ago, dared to go places other women were hesitant to go, dared to say things other women were hesitant to say, and by the very way she lived, confronted men to be more of who they were created to be.

Not that this ordinary woman's life had failed to affect my own personal journey as I walked with her and her remarkable husband, Doug.

Not that I had failed to seek out this ordinary couple when I was in a season of oppression. I needed them to use their experience to probe me to see if I had in some way opened a door for the enemy attacks I was experiencing.

Not that I had failed to walk in even more depth with this ordinary couple and their extraordinary God as we traveled together to Asia and made repeated journeys into China, distributing Bibles and study materials to our persecuted family of believers in Jesus.

Glory!

But I was still unprepared to be as impacted and challenged as I was in the reading of this book. Here were journeys about which I knew nothing. I love the way this "ordinary woman" held tenaciously to the words and promises of Jesus—words that made her unafraid in multiple otherwise scary situations. I love the way she resolutely held on to Jesus' words regarding healing when medical diagnoses would predict permanent disability or even death. She refused to relegate Jesus' words to the bins of history but accepted them as words for the day and found the Lord faithful in the fulfillment of those promises.

I recommend this book to every serious-minded follower of Jesus. I can almost promise that you will be challenged to dig deeper into your own life of faith, trusting Jesus for more.

Thank you, Drew, for recognizing that your mother's story needed to be told. Thank you for that extraordinary Christmas gift.

And thank you, Anne Severance, for the extraordinary way in which you have pulled these stories out of Dabney's memory and recorded them in a way that challenges all of us to lean more purposefully into "more of Jesus" that is ours for the taking.

—Don Finto
Pastor Emeritus, Belmont Church
Founder, Caleb Global

ACKNOWLEDGMENTS

My heart is filled with gratitude as I am reminded of all those who have been a part of this journey.

First is the Lord, who lights our paths and orders our steps, enabling the incredible and the impossible. Then, there is my beloved husband, Doug, my chief encourager and support; and our sons, Doug and Drew, who prayed for me and tolerated my absences for weeks at a time.

There were many who gave their pastoral oversight and encouragement. For Billy Roy Moore, Dwight Marable, Don Finto, Stephen Mansfield, Mick Antanaitis, David Hooper, Steve and Nancy Fry, Lindsay Wenth, Shannon McClaird, Jeff Dollar, Mickey Robinson, and James and Michal Ann Goll, I am eternally grateful.

Then, the host of stalwart-hearted women God called to walk together while experiencing His adventures and the joy of His manifest presence. James Goll named us the "Glory Girls."

The Lord gives the word [of power];
the women who publish [the news] are a great host.
The kings of enemies' armies, they flee, they flee.
She who tarries at home divides the spoils [left behind].
Psalm 68:11–12 AMPC

Special thanks to Barbie Graham, Artist, and Chelsea Phillips, Worship Leader and Graphic Artist—among the original Glory Girls—for creating the cover of *GLORY!*

Glory!

Finally, my everlasting gratitude to Anne Severance, who has taken these stories, treated them as holy, and has woven a tapestry with words.

My undying gratitude to all.

—Dabney

INTRODUCTION

It was to be a surprise for my mom. A Christmas gift, actually—tucked under the tree in an out-of-the-way spot so as not to be noticed right away. To be opened after all the others were admired and enjoyed for a bit. Wrapped in ordinary paper and tied with a crinkly, well-worn bow.

There had been grander gifts. A car once. Dad's truck. I loved nothing more than to think of over-the-top ways to put a smile on their faces after all they had done for me—and for so many over the years.

But this one was different. Presented in a plain white box, beneath some tissue paper, was a vintage book. At least the *cover* of a book. Inside was the surprise: One hundred. Blank. Pages.

"But . . . but what *is* this?" Mom was clueless, no doubt wondering what on earth I was up to now.

"It's *your* book, Mom," I gently explained. "The one you're going to write. The one where you'll tell about your adventures all these years—smuggling Bibles to the persecuted Christians in China and all over the world. The Lord told me to hire a ghost-writer to help—"

Before I could finish my sentence, it was Dad who burst into tears. "It's what I've prayed for, honey! What I've always wanted you to do!"

And that's how it all began . . .

—Drew Mann

Glory!

i

That Christmas morning, when the last gift from Drew had been unwrapped, I sat in silence for a moment. Not that I wasn't touched by his thoughtfulness. My husband was actually in tears. But I wasn't sure how to respond. The last thing I would ever want to do is to write a book…about *me!* There is nothing to commend me except the grace of God.

Still, if I could somehow encourage others—especially the younger women—to hear Holy Spirit for themselves, then take up the torch and carry it into our darkening world, maybe I could try to share what the Lord has done with one ordinary wife and mom who loves Him with a passion that has not diminished in all these years.

Mary, the mother of Jesus, said it first and best at a wedding reception when the host ran out of wine for his guests. She knew her Son would have the solution. He always did. To the servants, she instructed, "Whatever He tells you to do, do it!" Not surprisingly—to her, at least—the second serving of wine was far better than the first.

Borrowing Mary's words, I could wrap up this book in one sentence, or maybe two: "Whatever He tells you to do, do it! Wherever He tells you to go, GO!" And thus begins my story of one divine assignment after another…and some of the testimonies of the people God has sent to go with me….

—Dabney Mann

Chapter 1

Here Am I…Send Me?

I heard the voice of the LORD, saying:
"Whom shall I send, and who will go for Us?"
Then I said, "Here am I! Send me."
Isaiah 6:8

Striking out into the unknown has never been a problem for me. For one thing, it hasn't occurred to me to consider the outcome in advance. Nor have I found it necessary to know every step in the process of reaching my destination. God says, "Go!" and I go—wherever and whenever there is a need and He opens a door.

That kind of response to His call may partly be because of my family's military background. My dad was a career naval officer during the 1940s and 1950s, and moving from place to place—whether in the States or abroad—was routine for as long as I can remember. Just any day, Mom might tell us kids, "Pack your bags. We're moving to Virginia Beach" or "Key West, Florida" or "San Mateo, California." Since Dad was in charge of military transportation for the Western Pacific Fleet for several years, "home" was often as far away as Tokyo and Yokohama, Japan, or Manila, Philippines.

Although my father seldom spoke of it, he helped to rescue people while stationed in Manila where he commanded the U.S.

Navy port. He often volunteered on weekends to fly to Bangkok to oversee an operation liberating the Vietnamese escaping the tyranny of communism in North Vietnam. The refugees would board LSTs (Landing Ship Tanks)—ships designed during World War II to transport troops and weapons directly onshore. Rather than heavy artillery, though, these people brought all their worldly possessions, including chickens and goats. What little I heard my dad say about these forays made a lasting impression on my young heart, and apparently the mantle of rescuing the helpless and oppressed passed to me.

Nevertheless, I didn't hear about God, His Son Jesus, or the Holy Spirit at home, and we were not church goers. In fact, my first impression of Jesus Christ came in my fifth-grade geography class. That year, we studied the South American country of Brazil. One illustration in our textbook touched me deeply—*Christ the Redeemer*—a monument erected high atop the Andes Mountains overlooking Rio de Janeiro. It was the towering figure of a Man with His arms outstretched as if He wanted to hug the whole world. Although I knew nothing about Jesus' true identity beyond that picture, in my ten-year-old mind, I figured that His kind of love could change everything, and we wouldn't have war anymore if enough people just learned how to love like that.

With my father in the military, my mother having received her master's degree in library science from the University of Virginia, and with a slew of lawyer uncles, I often overheard spirited political debates around our dinner table. After seeing the picture of the Man in my geography book, I felt I knew the answer to all those wars and uprisings.

So strong was my belief that I decided to address Congress and tell them all about this Christ—in case they hadn't heard. And I wouldn't wait around until I was a grown-up either. Determined to walk all the way to Washington, DC, from my home in Newport, Rhode Island, where Dad was stationed at the time, I set out with one goal in mind. To tell some of the most important people in our country about Someone who could stop wars and bring peace and love to everyone in every nation.

Without questioning the distance, I began my journey with this message burning in my heart. I later learned that the Capitol building, where the Congress met to pass laws, was over four hundred miles away and six and a half hours by car, and I was on foot. I had not gone far, of course, before I was "apprehended" by a nice policeman and returned to my frantic parents. That trip might have been aborted, but the seed of "saving the world" was firmly planted in the fertile soil of a little girl who would grow up with a mission to tell as many people as possible about the Man in whose Father's house they would be safe forever.

It would be many years before I would understand my true mission, though, much less the God who had created me to be a warrior for Him.

The Young and the Restless

To tell the truth, despite the apparent excitement of our frequent relocations—exploring new vistas—we were never in one spot long enough to form lasting friendships. Friends came into our lives only to be left behind with the next move. Thus, the feeling of isolation. Fear crept in, too, with its tentacles of uncertainty and insecurity whenever Dad was deployed to another global hot spot or some unfamiliar place in the States where we had to start all over again.

In one city where we moved while I was still in the elementary grades, I attended a Catholic convent school. Traditionally, students were given weeks of instruction and practice prior to their first communion, which would represent their official entry into the Catholic Church. As a little girl in the third grade, all the trappings of Catholicism—the rituals, the images, the pomp and pageantry—appealed to me, and what I saw, I wanted.

In my mind, I believed God must really love the Catholics if they would go to all that trouble for Him, and I wanted to be one of them. But my parents would not allow it. So I stole some statues of Jesus, Mary, and Joseph, some rosaries and medals of saints. I figured if I put Jesus under my bed, surely He could find me and be my Friend. Unfortunately, the good sisters were not so forgiving, and I was suspended from the school.

Later, there were all the hormonal highs and lows that accompany puberty, leading to self-image issues and, ultimately, wrong choices. I came to believe the lies, and I had no idea how to find the truth. In fact, I lied as a way of life—made stuff up—just to have something interesting to say.

I was a mess. A total mess.

———

As time passed, I became curious about my roots. Maybe some long-ago forefather would give me a clue as to why I was wired the way I was. A little research into the family tree turned up the fascinating information that among my Scottish ancestors was Sir James Douglas, known as the Black Douglas, loved by the Scots and feared by the British. Sir James fought gallantly alongside the king of the Scots, Robert the Bruce, in the battle for Scottish independence. According to the custom of the day, upon the king's death, it was a knight—in this case, my forebear Sir James—who carried his king's heart into the Crusade with the Moors in Spain.

There was also a random entry in my maternal great-great-grandmother's diary in which she referred to "Cousin John Knox." The world-famous theologian and leader of the Scottish Reformation was my distant *cousin*?! This dual source of my later burning desire for things of God must have come down through the generations—on both sides of the family. So, my legacy *wasn't* dark and foreboding. Still, I was clueless in my early years.

In fact, my only ambition in those days was to become a grown-up. Grown-ups could do what they wanted, whenever they wanted—go anywhere they wanted. And "Go" was my middle name.

When the time came for me to connect with the real Source of my pent-up passion and fire, I would say to the King of kings something similar to the declaration made by my kinsman, John Knox, "Give me Scotland . . . or I die!" My twenty-first-century version of this petition would be "Lord, give me the *nations* . . . or I die!"

I wasn't thinking such lofty thoughts as a young girl, however. Much time would pass before I accepted the divine call. Meanwhile, other things occupied my mind.

Wedding Belle

The hours seem to drag when you're young, just waiting for the day when you are free to fly. Like so many others, I could hardly wait to leave the nest for that great adventure called life. To be honest, though, I had few preconceived ideas as to what that would look like for me. I only knew that, despite our frequent moves, *then* would surely be more exciting than *now*.

So, it was a step in the right direction when I left for Erskine College in South Carolina. One interesting observation I made during my college career was the favor I seemed to have from my male classmates. I was no beauty queen, so it was always a bit of a mystery. But despite five proposals in my senior year, it was not a college guy who won my heart. It was a young man I had met when my sister's date brought him along to the house one Fourth of July to meet me. His name was Doug, and we dated off and on for the next five years. And thus began the first chapter of a lifelong love story.

I remember where I was standing in the parking lot of my summer school campus in July 1964, when I felt a distinct nudge from the One I scarcely knew at the time. It was as if the Lord Himself spoke to me in words something like this: *If you don't marry Doug Mann, your life will not turn out the way I intended.*

Since I have never been one to sit around twiddling my thumbs, things ramped up quickly. A few days later, I broke the news to Doug that we should get married as soon as possible. It was against university policy for married students to remain in school and I had another year at Erskine, so we would have to keep our marriage a secret for a while. Besides, if I didn't listen to this gentle whisper—strangely, a voice I had heard before—something might happen, and it wouldn't get done. Being the same kind of risk-taker I am, Doug took me up on my suggestion immediately, and I didn't have to talk him into it.

We knew each other pretty well by now, so this was no hasty decision on my part. Besides, he was "an older man"—by four years, to be exact—and had worked on his dad's cattle ranch in Florida for a while before landing a job in the finance department of a loan company. Mature, experienced, and employed. I figured that would satisfy my dad, since my plumbline for a potential husband had always been "someone my father could respect."

So, on a sun-drenched morning in September, I grabbed a floral print shirtwaist dress and some Bass Weejuns and stuffed them into my purse. We made the four-hour trip from Tampa to Folkston, Georgia—just over the Georgia line—where the three-day waiting period was not required.

Spotting a sign that read "Blood Tests, $5.00! High Test, 28 cents!" we pulled into a parking spot. Strangely enough, the site happened to be a gas station. But Doug and I weren't picky. Once we had our instant results as promised, we took the report to the county courthouse, where a justice of the peace performed a civil ceremony, and we made the return trip to Tampa with none the wiser.

Of course, there was no honeymoon. I went back to school

and Doug to work as if nothing had happened that would affect the rest of our lives, I was now Mrs. Douglas Mann, although no one would ever know that we had tied the knot before our formal wedding several months later, in February 1965. Well, now *you* know.

———

Doug: Dabney and I had been married for only a couple of months when my father invited us to join him on a fishing expedition to the Everglades National Park. He had recently purchased a fine new boat and was eager to try it out. Young and adventurous, my new wife and I were on.

Upon arrival at the agreed-upon location—Flamingo City near the Shark River—we drove to the river's edge and helped Daddy unhitch the boat from the trailer. It slid easily into the water. No sharks, but there was always the strong possibility of alligators lurking silently beneath the surface.

We motored out a distance from the shoreline, attached the fishing lures to our rods, and cast our lines into the dark, tea-stained river, steeping in the roots of giant cypress trees lining the bank.

Inadvertently, at some point, my fishing rod was knocked into the water. Desperate to retrieve it before it was swept away by the tidal current, I dove in. When I opened my eyes underwater, I could barely see my hand in front of my face. How was I ever going to find my gear now?

A split-second later, I heard the sound of someone diving in behind me. It was Dabney, ready to help in the hunt.

When we finally resurfaced—minus the missing rod—and hoisted ourselves into the boat, my father studied my wife with obvious admiration. "Son, you've really landed yourself a good one. She's a keeper. Utterly fearless!"

I took another look at my beautiful bride. I knew she was special, but I was just beginning to realize how *special. Daddy was right.*

This girl was not afraid of anything—not dark waters, undetermined depths, or alligators. In those early days, I had no way of knowing that her courage in the face of unknown dangers would stand her in good stead in all the challenging years ahead.

Looking for the Lover of My Soul

I thought I had found the one thing I was looking for when I married Doug—true love. And I had. The earthly kind. But there was still a yearning within me for something more—much, much more.

In college, I had taken courses in both the Old and New Testaments. But my professors never explained that God loved me or that He had sent His Son Jesus to save me from my sins. I figured you were born either "bad" or "good," and there was nothing you could do to change it.

Reading the Bible left me completely confused. It seemed that God was mad at all the bad people one day—even the religious types—yet talking about love and compassion the next. I just couldn't figure Him out. I never heard the terms *born again* or *saved* or *baptism of the Holy Spirit*. Didn't know that Jesus had already done all the work—if I would only believe in Him and repent of my sins. All I knew was that I wanted God—and I didn't know how to find Him.

Then something happened that gave me a little hope. Having moved into the first home we had purchased in Tampa, Florida—one of seven corporate moves in six years—we had started attending an Episcopal church. Still looking for God, I was drawn to a prayer meeting held there in the mornings. I kept going back again and again, hoping to find the missing link. What else did I have to do to connect with this elusive God and His Son? And what about His mysterious Holy Spirit?

Living in different cities, we rarely saw Doug's older sister Bootsie except on holidays. At Christmas that year, Bootsie had been her volatile self—cold and distant one moment and given to angry outbursts the next. By Easter, when we gathered again as a family, there had been a radical transformation. She was not the same person.

"I've been baptized in the Holy Spirit," she explained, radiating a peace and joy we had never seen in her.

So, it is *possible to change,* I thought. Whatever had happened to Bootsie, I wanted it.

———

By now, we had welcomed our first son into our hearts—Douglas Randall Mann. On his first birthday, I was planning to mow the lawn. I started the mower, but unfortunately, my foot was under it. Before I knew it, I had lopped off part of my big toe.

Bleeding and in pain—and with Doug at work—I drove myself to the nearest drug store.

"Lady, you don't need a Band Aid," the pharmacist said after examining the wound, "you need a surgeon."

The moment I hopped inside the door of Dr. William Standish Reed's office, I felt something almost tangible. The very atmosphere was saturated with the indescribable essence of something I had never experienced before. I had not met any of these people—the doctor, the nurses, the receptionist, the office manager—yet for the first time, I sensed that they all truly cared . . . that they *loved* me.

I had heard Bootsie's testimony about the Holy Spirit. Something like "unseen, yet very present; powerful, yet tender as a mother's touch." Was this what I was feeling now? Whatever it was—whoever *He* was—I couldn't wait to get back to this place of unconditional love.

The day I had the stitches out, the doctor's wife was in the office. A beautiful woman, she too was warm and caring. I was told that right after office hours, the two of them were heading to a Full Gospel Businessmen's Conference. They were Christians—people who knew God personally. So *that* was why they were so happy all the time, so full of love.

And then something clicked. I had been reading a book by a Reverend Dennis Bennett—*Nine O'Clock in the Morning.* Bennett had written that the Bible says that is the time of day when the first Christians "received the Holy Spirit." Not having read the Bible for myself, I knew next to nothing about God's Spirit. Was this some kind of holy mist that hovered around God? And now around Bootsie?

Somewhere in his book, the author, living in the Far West at the time, mentioned that he had a brother-in-law, a surgeon, who lived in Tampa, Florida. His name? William Standish Reed. Was the Holy Spirit what I had felt in Dr. Reed's office that day? *Maybe Christians who have "received the Holy Spirit" give off a certain aura, something like a heady perfume*, I thought. It appeared that I might be a few steps closer to ending my search. Only an all-knowing, loving Being could connect the dots like this.

God works in mysterious ways.

Finding Jesus . . . and Something More

Doug's transfer from Tampa to Atlanta brought a whole new dimension to my quest to find my destiny in God. Typical of the Old South, a neighbor came to call almost before we had unpacked and settled in. With a little boy of four and a toddler, I knew the settling in would take a bit longer than usual.

"Welcome to At-*lan*-ta!" The woman at my doorstep simply oozed Southern charm. Without waiting for a reply, she went on, "Oh, are you a Christian?" She had obviously spotted the Bible on our coffee table.

"Um, no," I replied hesitantly. Under my breath, I added, "But I want to be. I just don't know how."

I had given Doug the Bible as a wedding gift. Why I had

chosen that particular gift, I really didn't know since neither of us were believers.

My new neighbor had no idea of the story that Bible could tell. I had been seven months pregnant at the time of the Tampa tornado of 1966. With Doug away at work, I was home alone, lying on a couch in the living room when tornadic winds had ripped through our duplex and blown away everything, including our bed. Only Doug's Bible was left. "Oh, God, please save my baby!" I had cried out—the first unselfish prayer I had ever prayed.

He answered uniquely, through a Sikh professor at the University of South Florida who lived across the street. Bruised and dazed—yet lucky to be alive—I got to my feet, live wires sending sparks into the air from downed power lines around me. I distinctly remember seeing the Indian professor in his turban, carefully working his way through the debris to help me to safety.

The incident was not without consequences. Within a week, the trauma caused toxemia, and I could have lost the baby and perhaps my own life.

Before I could speak again, my neighbor—who had looked at me like she didn't know what to do with me—hurried on, "I know what we can do. There's a neighborhood Bible study tonight if you're interested. I know a great sitter for your kids. Would you like to come?"

I couldn't get there fast enough. And by 7:30, my new friend and I were walking through another neighbor's back door.

"Hey! Come on in!" greeted our hostess, waving us into her kitchen. "You're just in time. God is growing out legs tonight. Everyone is downstairs."

Whaat?! Was this some kind of crazy house? But I was so determined to find what I was looking for, I didn't care. Maybe "growing out legs" was what God did in His spare time.

We followed her to the basement where a group of people

had gathered, sweet tea glasses and Bibles in hand. At the front of the room was a man wearing white shoes and red socks. He had a Texas accent, and I later learned he was an itinerant preacher.

A glance around the room assured me that all limbs seemed to be intact and the proper length, so *that* part of the evening must have concluded. Still, I desperately wanted what all these people seemed to have—an incredible peace, yet an excitement that was almost palpable.

I'm not sure that I recall everything our speaker had to say that evening, but when he finished, he added, "If you need something from God tonight, turn to someone on your left and ask for prayer."

Immediately, I turned to the young man on my left and said, "I want to be baptized in the Holy Spirit."

"Uh . . . not sure I can help you there," he admitted. "I think you'd better talk to the preacher."

I wasted no time in getting down front, and repeated my request.

"When were you saved?" the pastor asked.

Of course, I had no real understanding of the meaning of *saved*, so I muttered something in reply, upon which the man put one hand on my head and began to pray. Before either of us could blink, I was praying in a language I had never heard before!

How odd of God that He should take a young woman with no biblical knowledge at all and fill her so full of Himself that she would spill over in a holy utterance in front of a group of strangers. And oh, what joy! In that moment, all the pieces fit: God, the Father; Jesus, His Son, our Savior; and even the "mystical" Holy Spirit, God's Presence and Power. Three in One. Each with His distinctive personality, yet One True and Living God.

Years later, while ministering to some Buddhists in Tibet, I remembered that night in Atlanta. I learned how the Buddhist monks produce beautiful sand paintings by dropping handfuls of painted sand into an artistic pattern, commingling the different colors into one glorious collage. In retrospect, that was the vision the Father had given me in my neighbor's basement. No wonder I was euphoric and could not stop praising Him, singing non-stop. He had given me all of Himself in one moment of time.

When I finally got home, I didn't tell Doug what had happened to me. How could I begin to explain that I was saved, filled with the Holy Spirit, and now speaking in tongues—all in one night? But later that week, he overheard me confiding the whole scenario to a friend on the phone.

I might have expected a negative response from him or a warning about jumping too quickly into something that seemed weird. At least, something about which we had little knowledge or experience.

Instead, when I hung up from that phone conversation, he hugged me tight. "I'm so proud of you, honey," he said.

Wonders never cease.

"Just Take it All!"

My newfound faith must have been contagious. It wasn't long before Doug took that step after hearing an Episcopal priest—the only evangelist in the entire denomination—teach on the baptism of the Holy Spirit in a series of weekend meetings. My husband wanted what I had—the irrepressible joy, the deep peace and contentment. But most of all, he wanted the enabling power of the Holy Spirit to do what we cannot do.

It was while we were serving coffee at the fellowship following one service that I knew Doug's experience was deep and true. That evening, a roomful of people had gathered to share personal testimonies about what God had done for them. One lady stood and tearfully proclaimed, "I went home after the meeting last night and prayed for my children." Still young in the faith, my first impression was that the priest's teaching had merely triggered an emotional response in her.

Just then, a nice young man wearing a suit spoke up. "A friend picked me up at the airport a couple of hours ago. He told me about this meeting, and I felt I was supposed to come. But I didn't understand why . . . until now. You see, that lady who just stood to speak . . . is my stepmother. I haven't seen her in eight years."

Doug leaned over and, in an excited whisper, said to me, "Dabney, this stuff is *real!*"

Obviously moved by what had taken place, Doug knelt in the back of the church and prayed, "Okay, I give up. I give You my life. I give You my house . . . my job . . . my car. But please don't send me to Ethiopia as a missionary." He paused, then added, "Oh, what the hell. Just take it all!"

That pretty much summed it up for both of us. The Holy Spirit was real, and we were ready and willing to give it all to Him and let Him lead us. Only a week later, we opened our home to a small group of those who had also been touched in these meetings. Of the forty to sixty people who showed up at our door that first Tuesday night, at least four of them begged for prayer. There was not room in our house for so many, so we spilled out onto the lawn. But we were so new at all this.

Setting the Captives Free

Before we knew it, we were praying for the salvation and deliverance of a steady stream of people, many of whom we had never met before. Out of the blue, the phone would ring or there would be a knock at the door, and they would come—the hopeless, the helpless, those tormented by demonic spirits. What in the world did we know about the kingdom of darkness? We would learn soon enough.

Doug: *What happened next was as much a surprise to us as to anyone else. My own deliverance happened under the teaching of international Bible scholar Derek Prince, along with about 130 others at a Holiday Inn during a weekend seminar. I was sitting in the audience,* *minding my own business, when I heard a strange wailing sound coming from what I supposed was the loudspeaker system. Found out it was the groaning of demonically tortured souls on the front row. Before I knew it, I had joined in the howls and moans as strongholds I didn't even know existed, lifted from me. I felt ten pounds lighter.*

After that, we knew nothing more than to follow the clear instruction of our Deliverer. His last recorded words in the Gospel of Mark are these: "In My name they [those who believe] will drive out demons" (16:17). "In My name"—that's Jesus! "Those who believe"—that's us!

Yet, a question commonly asked among believers is this: "Can a Christian be possessed by demons?" The answer is an emphatic no. Possession implies ownership, and Christians are owned by Jesus. But demons can definitely influence believers. Like the Holy Spirit who operates within us to conform us to the image of Jesus (love, joy, peace, patience, kindness, gentleness, goodness, faithfulness, and self-control), demons or evil spirits work to conform us to their image (fear, anger, murder, lust, discouragement, depression, etc.).

One of the primary roles of a Christian, we learned, is to confront demonic powers and set the captives free. The Lord expects us to take an aggressive, combative stance against these evil spirits as we follow His commands. In other words, Dabney and I simply took Him at His word and hoisted the sails, and the Holy Spirit blew.

Word spread and the media picked up on our unusual activity. We were interviewed on television and featured in the local newspaper. A reporter shot a photo of us in which we looked like "normal" people. But back then, our story—taking the gospel outside the walls of the church and into the marketplace—might have been something of a first.

United Press International got wind of the story and it landed on the front page of a Knoxville paper, with the headline reading: "Banker by Day, Exorcist by Night!" Certainly nothing we would have planned, but perhaps a novel way of promoting the gospel of Jesus Christ and the power of His Spirit. And for the next ten years, three nights each week, we met with a total of over a thousand tortured souls, leading them out of the darkness of Satan's domain and into the sweet freedom of God's powerful love and forgiveness.

Fortunately, when people started coming to us for prayer and ministry, we had some idea of how to help. Doug had taken copious notes during Derek Prince's sessions, recording everything he could scratch down. He would read through his notes and, simply stated, we would put the teaching into practice. Supported by the Scriptures Dr. Prince had listed, we believed what Jesus said, then did what He did . . . and people were delivered. (Much more about this later.)

Soon, we were praying not only for those in our group and those who showed up at our door, but for the nations. In the process of prayer, we were led to give—time, money, and teaching—and then to go. And, I learned, it would begin with the nation nearest God's own heart: Israel.

Chapter 2

To Israel, with Love

"I will bless those who bless you,
and I will curse him who curses you;
and in you all the families of the earth will be blessed."
Genesis 12:3

My heart for Israel blossomed about two months after I was saved. Doug and I had been reading *The Late Great Planet Earth* by Hal Lindsay. After finishing the last page, we were so convicted that Doug wrote a check to the *Jerusalem Post,* Israel's most-read English newspaper. It was our intention to keep up with what was happening in the Middle East with the Chosen People. If God Himself had marked their boundaries and set them apart from all other nations, they must be really special.

In the early 1970s, as new believers hungry for the Word, we had listened to the teachings of Derek Prince. Although he was born in India and educated in England, ultimately teaching in a prestigious university, this man's love for Israel was evident, and he frequently emphasized its biblical importance to "grafted-in" Christians. In fact, Dr. Prince had lived in Israel for several years, had attended the Hebrew University in Jerusalem, and had met his first wife, Lydia, there.

It was Dr. Prince who taught us to "pray for the peace of Jerusalem" and to support the Jewish people in view of the continuing rise of antisemitism. It would be a few years before we would meet this man personally and enjoy a tour of Israel with him, soaking in every precious moment of discovery.

When we visited a church in Nashville—Belmont Church, led by a pastor who later became a close friend, Don Finto—we were further enlightened about our responsibility to the Jewish people. On one occasion, we heard a guest speaker who was the curator of the Garden Tomb in Jerusalem. The chief takeaway from his message was, "Make a friend of a Jewish person."

As we walked back to the car after the service, Doug said, "I believe we heard the word of God today. But we just can't walk up to a Jewish person and say, 'Will you be my friend?'"

He was right. We didn't know a single Jewish person in the entire city. But if this was God's heart, we wanted to. And we began to pray, "Lord, we don't know any Jewish people. Please send us someone."

In February 1976, while in church at the Lord's Chapel, Doug and I had noticed an older couple who appeared to be from another country. Despite their origin, they seemed to know all the songs we were singing from mimeographed song sheets. (That, of course, was in the days before high-tech screens, worship teams, and fog machines.)

After the service, the dignified lady walked over to introduce herself. "Hello, I'm Lillian Hook," she said with a distinctively British accent. We learned that she was an eminent archaeologist who had participated in every dig in Israel since 1939. Astounding!

We made small talk until Pastor Billy Roy Moore approached to greet her. During the course of the conversation, he invited Dr. Hook to share with the church at a later date. Of course, Doug and I made plans to be there. We couldn't wait to see what God had up His sleeve this time.

On that evening, Dr. Hook told the audience about her first impression of the Jewish people and how they were regarded. As early as the first grade, she had noticed that Jewish children were treated with contempt by the other children. When she asked her father about this, he only remarked sadly, "The whole world hates the Jews."

"Well," she said, drawing herself up to her full six-year-old height, *"I'll* be their friend. And so I have all these years.

"May I say that you Americans have done two things well," she continued. "First, you have sent or carried the gospel to Israel and, for that matter, to virtually every nation. Second, you have stood with Israel politically and blessed her. We have all lived to see this Scripture [Isaiah 66:8 TPT] fulfilled: 'Who has ever seen or heard of such a wonder? Could a country be born in a day? Can a nation be birthed so suddenly?'"

"Yet, on May 14, 1948, after David ben Gurion, head of the Jewish Agency, proclaimed the establishment of the State of Israel, your president, Harry S. Truman, was the first to recognize the new nation—on the same day!"[1]

Dr. Hook went on to make a prophetic declaration, although we didn't understand it at the time: "Just watch and see what God does in Israel on July 4, 1976—your bicentennial—to show that the destinies of the USA and Israel are tied together."

We already knew that Israel is the only nation that God had declared as His special people, His nation, while America is the only nation founded upon the premise that God is our God. In other words, God chose Israel; our founders chose God.

Blessing Israel

Early on the morning of July 5, Doug was at home. Our sons, Doug and Drew, were still asleep. We made a pot of coffee, spread the newspaper on the breakfast room table, and began to read. At the top of an inside page was the glaring headline: "Hijacked

Hostages' Rescue a Miracle, Sister Says."[2] The raid had taken place on the previous day, July 4, as predicted by Dr. Hook. Was this what our archaeologist acquaintance had been prophesying?

We read on: "In a stunning 36-minute midnight strike in Uganda, Israeli commandos rescued more than 100 hostages held by pro-Palestinian hijackers and flew triumphantly back to Tel Aviv yesterday."[3]

Since all the hostages were Israelis (Jews)—the Palestinians had released those of other nationalities—and the U.S. military had not aided in this midnight rescue, we could not imagine why the Lord had called our attention to it. Yet, our hearts were stirred, and somehow, we knew there was a connecting link. We only needed to read a little further to grasp it.

A few pages over, we read of a local celebration in honor of the freed hostages to be held that night at the West End Synagogue. The announcement stated: "All are invited!" We assumed that meant Gentiles as well as those from the Jewish community. No question about it; as unusual as it seemed in that day, we would be there in a show of support.

———

On the way to the synagogue, driving down I-65, Doug spoke up in a flash of inspiration. "Dabney, read Acts 2:17–18. I feel this is important."

I had my Bible with me and flipped over to the second chapter of Acts and began reading verse 17: "'And it shall come to pass in the last days,' says God, 'that I will pour out My Spirit on all flesh.'"

I would have read on, but Doug interrupted me. "Wait. Go back to that Joel passage: 2:28–32."

In these verses, I noted that the first words were exactly the same prophecy: "And it shall come to pass . . . I will pour out My Spirit on all flesh."

All flesh. With the inner knowing of when the Spirit speaks to our hearts, we knew that a much bigger picture was about to unfold.

"These Are My Friends!"

When we arrived at the synagogue, the place was packed. All of the attendees appeared to be Jewish people. Not another Christian in sight. Traditions unfamiliar to us were on full display. Shofars—Israeli trumpets—being blown. Dancing in the aisles. Banners waving. Had we done the wrong thing in assuming that it would be acceptable for us to be here?

Doug: I must admit I had my doubts, too, and then suddenly a lady walked over to greet me. I recognized her as a wealthy client of the bank. She and her husband, who owned one of the largest retail businesses in town, found it necessary to move their money around after banking hours. I was usually there to help.

Obviously puzzled, she frowned. "What are you doing here?"

"We're here to celebrate what the Lord has done."

Without warning, the lady clutched her chest, then slumped against the wall. If Dabney and I had not stepped closer to steady her on either side, she would surely have slid to the floor.

"Wh-what is this?" she asked in a whisper, her eyes wide. "What's happening to me?"

"It's the Lord pouring out His love on you," I reassured her.

Brightening, she straightened and called out to her husband, who was still chatting with some guys across the room. "Har-ree! Come over here!"

Harry—no more than five-feet-tall—rushed over as fast as his ample girth would allow. "What is it, dear?"

"I want you to meet my new friends."

Before the evening ended, we were introduced to several visiting rabbis, along with other leaders of the Jewish community. Surprisingly, I was invited to address a group of men at their regular monthly gathering at the old Jewish Community Center.

When the time came, I'm sure they were wondering why I, as a Christian, would support Israel. I sent up a one-word prayer to the Lord: "Help!" and the first question I was asked was an open invitation to spread more of God's love to His Chosen People: "What's all this about that 'born-again' business?"

With President Jimmy Carter running for office at the time and his self-avowed profession as a "born-again Christian," this phrase was familiar to the Jewish community, although not its meaning.

"Let me explain it this way," I began, "Jacob's name mirrored his character. The name means 'conniver, con artist, deceiver,' and so he was. But when he encountered God on the banks of the Jabbok River, his name and his character were changed from 'deceiver' to 'Israel, Prince of God.' From that day forward, he didn't walk the way he used to walk; he walked with a limp. When we encounter God, everything changes. We don't walk the way we used to walk; we walk with God, but we walk with a limp."

Before we adjourned, an older Jewish fellow came up to me and whispered in my ear: "That happened to me."

Like Dabney, I was touched by the history of these persecuted people and delighted in the knowledge that some of them were discovering true freedom in Christ, their Messiah.

On my fortieth birthday, I celebrated by writing letters to nine Russian embassies around the world, supporting the right of the Refuseniks—Russian Jews who wanted to emigrate to their homeland, Israel. My message to the ambassadors pretty much echoed Moses's declaration to Pharaoh: "Let my [God's] people go!"

I did what I could do. Dabney continued to do what she does so well.

"To Israel, with Love"

The bond forged that night at West End Synagogue did not end there with these dear Jewish people, some of whom we now called friends. Not long after that, I met Peggy Tohrner, a precious elderly lady who could no longer drive at night. So, often over the next several years, it was my pleasure to take her to the weekly shabbat meal and service at the synagogue.

On the way, I would take advantage of the opportunity to tell her how God feels about Israel, and she always listened with interest. So much so that she asked me to speak to a group of young women, prospective members of Hadassah—a compassionate organization of Jewish women who use their money and influence to improve medical and educational facilities in Israel, forward Zionist activities in the United States, and promote world peace.

I accepted, somewhat reluctantly at first. But I became more enthusiastic about the assignment when I realized that the Lord wanted to give more women a voice to speak for Him in our day. "Lord, what do you want me to say to them?" I asked.

As always, right on time, He gave me the message: "Tell them that I love them and that I will keep every promise I have ever made to Israel. I will bring My people from the four corners of the earth—from the north, the south, the east, and the west. Russia will have to give up those she has held captive, and multitudes will return to their homeland—the land I promised them."

I went on to tell them more about the nature of God—His great mercy, grace, and compassion for all people. Apparently, the message fell on receptive ears, and every single prospective member joined Hadassah that day. In addition, I was invited to become a lifetime member of this organization and a member of the board, with my particular assignment to keep up with news from Israel and to give a monthly report at board meetings. To stay in even closer touch, I volunteered to work in the Hadassah thrift shop each week. With each contact, our bonds of love and understanding grew richer and deeper.

———

It was about that time, in the mid-1980s, when a Jewish woman named Jane Eskind was running for governor of Tennessee. She had been invited to address the women of the Jewish community at a luncheon. For some reason, she had to cancel, and I was asked to fill in.

When I arrived at the temple, the women were all dressed to the nines—hats, elegant dresses, and I even spotted a mink-lined raincoat. The tables were adorned with fresh flowers and lovely place settings of fine china and silver. Among the well-dressed women were a few men, some of them rabbis.

As usual, I asked the Lord what He would have me say to this distinguished gathering. This time, the answer was abundantly clear. I knew about the persecuted church in China, and it had pierced my heart. Now, I was to pass on to my Jewish friends what I had learned.

My audience—some of whom still bore on their forearms the tattooed numbers of the Nazi concentration camps—had never heard of such a thing. They were spellbound as the truth gradually dawned on them. Gentile or Jew—evil is no respecter of persons or nationalities.

But there was more. "Over forty years ago, a dear friend wrote an apology to the Jewish people in the language of my own heart," I said. "I'd like to share it with you now. It is titled 'To Israel, with Love.'

"Her apology reads: "'In the past, we like many "traditional Christians" accepted false teachings concerning God's covenant relationship with the Jewish people. We were wrong and ask forgiveness for centuries of ignorance and arrogance.

"'As God has begun to place His Spirit within us and allowed us to touch His heart, our eyes have been opened to see and even experience the precious and steadfast love God has for His beloved Israel.

"'We are indebted to you for our deep spiritual roots and acknowledge that our acceptance by the Holy One of Israel is nothing less than a merciful gift. We are blessed to be in the family of God.'

"My friend ended her tribute with your beautiful word for peace, *shalom*. I would like to add that we Gentiles have never replaced Israel—that is, taken your place at the table, silverware, china, and all—as some have suggested. We who love and honor the God of Abraham, Isaac, and Jacob stand with you against the forces of darkness. As the Scriptures have foretold, we are one new man. I, too, am blessed to be in the family of God. *Shalom*."

⸺

Time passed, and on an unexpected trip to China, I recall being on a boat on the famed Li River, one of the ten "watery wonders of the world." Observing its serene beauty, I felt as if I were enclosed in a bubble—alone with the Lord. My heart was once again stirred for the Jewish people. Feeling a pang in my spirit as I realized that one trip to China would never be sufficient to meet the needs of the brothers and sisters in Christ who were forced to worship underground or face imprisonment or even torture and death for their faith, I wept. For three days I wept.

Our leader thought I was having a nervous breakdown, and I couldn't tell him I wasn't. In fact, I didn't know what was happening to me. In retrospect, I know it was an "alabaster box moment" as I poured out everything at the feet of Jesus. Submitting to the tug in my heart, I prayed, "Lord, You know I will go anywhere, anytime, to tell Your story—but what about Israel?"

I will never forget His answer to me: *Israel is Mine, but I give you China.*

Chapter 3

I Give You China!

"Blessed are those who are persecuted
for righteousness' sake,
for theirs is the kingdom of heaven."
Matthew 5:10

I remember exactly where I was sitting in church that Sunday in 1984—on the front row, the row reserved not for the elite but for the hungry. I was feasting on the words that would shape the rest of my life after the most powerful worship I had ever encountered.

Our speaker that day was Dwight Marable, founder and president of Missions International. Dwight had recently returned from a trip around the world to see what God was doing in the nations. His report on China shocked my soul.

"There are 50 million Chinese Christians practicing their faith underground," he began, "and 48 million of them do not have a Bible."

That statistic alone was staggering, but there was more.

"Bibles are hand-copied, and in many villages, there is only one Bible for all the villagers to share. On our trip around the world, we carried $300, raised by some of the children in your congregation, to Hong Kong for Bibles to be printed in the

Chinese dialects. Reverend Dennis Balcombe, a pastor and apostle to the underground church who was once smuggled across the border in a casket, made a statement I have never forgotten. I quote him now," Dwight said, pausing to scan the crowd. "'Hadn't you rather *go* than send money?'"

His piercing gaze met mine, and it seemed he was addressing his question directly to me. I knew the answer without a moment's hesitation. *If what he is saying is true, I have to go. Those people are my brothers and sisters in Christ—my family.*

I glanced over at Doug for confirmation. From his expression, he was obviously not receiving the same message.

Doug: I saw the look in her eyes. I'd seen that look before—conviction coupled with firm resolve. On the way home from church, I asked her about it. "Something hit you today, didn't it? You're really into this."

"Yes," she said simply. Nothing more. No begging. No pleading. No demands or tearful petitions.

It was only later, after hearing that Dwight Marable was assembling a team to take Bibles into China, that Dabney quietly asked, "Can I go?"

"Sure, honey," I said, as much to placate her as anything, figuring she would soon drop the subject.

But the answer came for me, swiftly and suddenly, in the most unexpected of places—a Hallmark gift shop. With our twentieth anniversary coming up, I needed a card for Dabney, and that is what had brought me into this particular shop in the mall. While there, I decided that a milestone event like ours deserved more than a mere card and asked a clerk what gift she would suggest for a twentieth anniversary.

"Let me check," she said, smiling. "We have a list of traditional choices." She turned to a section behind the register, plucked a small catalog from the shelf, and ran her finger down the page. "Oh, here it is. For a twentieth anniversary, the suggestion is . . . china."

God's plan for Dabney was now crystal clear: She would be making the trip with Dwight and the team to China, where the persecution of Christians was a clear and present danger.

Saint and Smuggler

With this unusual opportunity, having Doug's blessing was important to me, as his business at the bank—and our family—would not allow him to get away to accompany me. In my mind, it wasn't his permission I needed, but his blessing. Not that I would have asked for it exactly. If it wasn't God's idea, I didn't even want to go.

In fact, if I hadn't been so sure that the trip to China was His mandate, I might have been a little skeptical. I was a nobody. No credentials. Inexperienced as a witness of the gospel. And, of course, I knew not one word of Chinese. That it could be dangerous for American Christians to take Bibles into an atheistic country never entered my mind.

Still, with the trip coming up in three weeks, I knew I had better find out how to pack and what to expect. But first, I needed to break the news to the boys—Doug Jr., now 17, and Drew, 14. I was a little concerned about their reaction since I was rarely separated from them—and certainly not at such a distance.

Drew was the son most impressed with my announcement. "Smuggling Bibles? You mean like Brother Andrew?" Drew had been reading Christian comics and had run across the story of this Dutch missionary who had smuggled Bibles into countries behind the Iron Curtain during the Cold War. "You mean, like *he* did—stashing Bibles under the floorboards of cars in Russia?"

He seemed thrilled with the idea that his mom, whose only previous claim to fame had been as a school crossing guard for the past five years, was possibly now going to become a notorious spy.

I recall the day I rose in Drew's estimation—at least, at that time in his young life when school was a big part of his world.

"Anyone interested in being a crossing guard for Harpeth Academy?" a friend had asked a group of us at lunch one day.

Hmm. With two boys enrolled in another private school, the money would come in handy. Besides, I had always wanted to be able to tithe my own personal income. "Yeah, *I* would," I replied.

As a school crossing guard—only one hour each school day—I would be directing traffic in and out of the school grounds and maintaining safety standards. Funny. Directing *anyone* to do *anything* is not my gift—and, as a little girl, I had only learned how to tell my right hand from my left by remembering which was my gun hand. *This should be interesting*, I thought. What I didn't know was that taking this job would also teach me a lesson in being ignored, demeaned, and disrespected. I was the unwelcome guest, ruining everyone's morning commute.

Why I had accepted the job, I'll never know. The truth is, I was so terrified standing in the middle of that busy street, all I could do was worship. I began to sing. No one could hear me since their car windows were rolled up. Nor could I hear their snide remarks. The more I sang, the more the Presence of God filled the atmosphere, and I began to love those drivers with their dirty looks. Soon I was smiling all the time. The birds, the squirrels . . . and Jesus. When we worship the Father, in His kindness He pours out His love.

For five years, during this hour each school day, I felt led to pray for Darryl Waltrip, who was a well-known NASCAR driver and drove this route every morning. Five years later, he accepted the Lord as his Savior and began hosting Bible studies in his home. Wonderful what God can do with one hour of prayer and praise!

Little did I know then that those years would be preparing me for the next exciting chapters in my life. After hearing Dwight Marable's impassioned plea for Christians in America to learn for themselves the plight of the persecuted church in China, I had felt an urgency to answer that call. And, as you know, Doug had finally gotten the message and granted his blessing. I was on my way. God would go with me.

Land of the Red Dragon

China. Land of mystery and intrigue. An ancient civilization with timeless contributions to the arts, science, and, in more recent decades, technology. A people yearning for truth and freedom yet muzzled by its repressive communistic government.

In a country with the nickname "The Red Dragon," I should have seen the analogy right away. Should have known that our little group—in attempting to bring the light of God's Word to the underground church in China—would be taking on the kingdom of darkness, the "red dragon" spoken of in John's Revelation (see 12:3–9).

Still, I really wasn't nervous.

One reason was the warp speed at which I had had to prepare for this trip, leaving little time for conjecture about what we would find upon arriving at our destination. I had been cautioned that we would be doing a lot of walking while tugging or carrying heavy luggage. To build muscle and endurance, Dennis Balcombe, who would be one of our guides in China, along with Dwight Marable, had encouraged us to train much like the Israeli army or our National Guard. Following his instructions, I started walking at least two or three miles at a time—with a five-pound bag of sugar in my backpack.

Meanwhile, well-meaning Christian friends criticized my decision to make this mission trip, wondering why I would take chances with my life when I had a husband and family to consider. What they didn't know was that much prayer had gone into this decision. And over a decade before that, Derek Prince had prayed over me, imparting a courage and determination that can only come from the Spirit of the Living God. Whatever He tells me to do, I will do—no matter who questions it. Besides, the Bible says that we must "obey God rather than man" (Acts 5:29).

Despite their dire warnings, I wasn't afraid.

That is, I wasn't nervous until I got there—not because I feared for my life, but because I didn't want to disappoint the Lord in failing to succeed at what He had sent me to accomplish.

First Stop—Hong Kong

Several couples from our church had signed up for this trip, about twenty-two of us altogether. We would pick up Dennis from his home in Hong Kong, along with the Bibles that were printed there in various dialects, and he would accompany us the rest of the way.

As I was hearing a bit about the people we would be visiting for the first time, I learned that the Chinese language, like the Hebrew, is a pictorial language. God's fingerprints are evident in the gospel message threaded throughout. For example, the symbol for *family* shows eight figures—the same number of people saved in Noah's ark during the great flood. The symbol for *garden* is a man, a woman, and a serpent. The symbol for *tree* is a cross. In so many of the Chinese "picture words," God is speaking to hearts, saying, "Come to Me! All of you from every tribe, tongue, and nation, come to Me!" I went to China, knowing that long ago, God had sent His Son ahead of our little group, and His sweet invitation was woven into the very fabric of the language the people spoke and wrote every day. The thought was exhilarating.

Our flight arrived on time, and we planned to connect with Dennis the next morning. On our first night in Hong Kong, that teeming city of over seven million people, a group of raucous Japanese teenagers pounded on the door of my hotel room, demanding to be let in. I recognized the language, having lived in Japan as a child when my father was stationed there. For a moment, I was terrified.

Before allowing fear to overwhelm me, I called the front desk to report the incident, then stepped to the door and began praying very loudly—in tongues! The group, intent on some kind of mischief no doubt, soon dispersed. Whew! First challenge tackled and overcome by my ever-present Helper.

With the Chinese authorities allowing only two Bibles per person entering their country, and with thousands of Bibles to distribute to the underground church, we had been instructed to wrap each of them in an item of clothing and pack them carefully in our suitcases. The X-ray machines used in the 1980s were unable to detect all the contents of a piece of luggage, especially if camouflaged in this way. Today, with our advanced technology, they would be able to count the number of aspirin tablets in a bottle.

Packed and prayed up, I slipped into bed, eager for the next day's adventure—my first foray into "enemy" territory. My last thought before sleep was, *We can do this—if You go with us, Lord.*

Border Crossing

Awake before dawn in this unfamiliar time zone, I hurriedly dressed in an olive-green jacket and slacks, unaware that this color, along with navy blue, was standard attire for Chinese officials and police officers. I would definitely blend in—well, except for my blond hair. Fortunately, Western tourists—that is, tourists who were not smuggling in contraband, such as Bibles—were welcome in this country at the time after years of isolation.

We received one warning, though: Our party of twenty must split up before crossing the border. Otherwise, if one was caught, all would be caught and the Bibles would be confiscated. I'll admit that losing sight of my companions while dragging the heavy suitcases would be a bit daunting, but I was determined. If God had commissioned this expedition, He would see us through. Our first objective, then, was to enter mainland China without being questioned.

At the border, there were many guards and many gates. So recent was the reopening of China to tourists (only five years earlier) that the "welcome stations" were still primitive. Barbed-wire fencing surrounded the area adjacent to a little river. A dirt path led to the main checkpoint, a makeshift plywood shack.

At this location, the guard studied my passport for what seemed an interminable length of time, then my face, before looking again at my passport. Would I be the first to fail inspection, thus causing our mission to be aborted? It was my worst nightmare.

Finally, after X-raying my luggage and finding nothing out of order, he stamped my passport, and I was free to enter. Suppressing a sigh of relief, I took my first step into the country that would claim my heart for the rest of my life.

"How Beautiful the Feet . . . "

After reaching our first destination—the White Swan Hotel in Guangzhou, formerly known as Canton, China—we had some time to catch our breath and get our bearings. The White Swan was a five-star luxury hotel where the nightly room rate was only $13 in American currency. Yet, how ironic that despite our impressive lodgings, the poverty level in the area was such that there was no trash in the streets. Most of the population in this city of over 15 million was too poor to throw away anything.

Guangzhou is situated on the banks of the Pearl River, a river that "ran red with the blood of the martyrs" during the Boxer Rebellion of 1900. We tried to mingle like other first-time tourists, but we were anything but ordinary tourists. Stowed in the luggage of each of the twenty people in our party were those illegal Bibles—two hundred of them per person—concealed as directed to avoid detection by the Secret Police.

In Hong Kong, we had been given duffel bags and huge barrel-shaped suitcases on rollers with combination locks where some of the Bibles would be placed, to be stored in the in-check rooms of the various facilities where we would stay. Members of the underground church would come to claim them, while other Bibles would be distributed in the Chinese provinces as we traveled throughout the country.

We had been warned about the police. Hotel rooms were wired, and conversations could be overheard and recorded. Therefore, we had to be careful not to incriminate any of the local Chinese believers in any way.

Before departing the United States, we had also been briefed on certain facts about the persecuted church in this area. At the time of the Boxer Rebellion, a group called the Society of Righteous and Harmonious Fists was formed to drive out all foreigners, including Chinese Christians. With our American culture of comfort and ease, we had little framework to support the real truth about the condition of believers in China. Only when Dennis smuggled a Chinese lady into a private hotel meeting room to share her story could I even *begin* to comprehend their plight.

She was a tiny little thing, a widow whose husband had died twenty-five years earlier in a communist prison camp. His crime? He was a believer who spoke English. Years of hard living lined her face. She was wearing typical Chinese attire—a navy blue cotton pantsuit and jacket with Mandarin collar. Everyone dressed alike in an effort to equalize according to the socialist agenda. But her feet! Oh, her feet! She wore socks that did not match, held in place by rubber bands. After her husband's death, she had walked from village to village to spread the gospel message among her people—for the past twenty-five years.

I knew then what I had to do. What the Holy Spirit was prompting me to do for this beloved ambassador of heaven. I had to wash her feet.

Hurrying to the restroom, I brought back a basin of water, some travel soap and lotion, and knelt to remove her mismatched socks. She backed away, shaking her head. "No, no! *I* should wash *her* feet!" she exclaimed in Chinese as Dennis translated.

I could barely see to tend to her for the tears in my eyes. These feet had carried her many a mile to proclaim God's love to her countrymen. This small thing was the least I could do.

As some of our team gathered around her, worship exploded in that room. We began to sing in the Spirit, and I am positive that angelic voices joined ours. Glorious!

———

A few days later, I encountered the Lord on that riverboat while on the Li River near Guilin. Overcome by my new understanding of the suffering of these believers and their enduring faith, tears again flowed freely—for three days. Torn between my call to Israel and this deeper revelation, I poured out my heart to God and received His. That is when God assured me that He had Israel in the palm of His hand, but He was giving me China. This would not be my last trip to the Land of the Red Dragon, after all.

Serving God in Shanghai

On this and subsequent trips to China, we would use all modes of transportation, sometimes traveling into smaller villages on trains, by car or bicycle, or even on foot, but for this leg of our journey, we flew into Shanghai. After we landed at midnight, we were instructed to transfer some of the Bibles from our luggage to duffel bags to be distributed to the underground church meeting in this province.

The problem was that with the terminal closed, our suitcases were dumped unceremoniously on the tarmac. Now, we had to locate our own gear in the darkness, remove the Bibles, and repack them in the duffel bags. With a bus waiting nearby, occupied by people who were likely ignorant of the gospel and might report us to the Secret Police, we had to make the transfer as quickly and as efficiently as possible. So as not to be observed, several of our party held out their big trench coats for cover while the rest of us worked feverishly.

After completing the task without detection, we boarded the bus, trying to blend in as discreetly as possible. For some reason known only to the passengers, they broke out in applause. It appeared that we were among friends, after all.

We traveled for several miles, and then we were dropped off in the middle of the road. What now? We started hitchhiking, but where we were headed, I had no idea. There were very few cars at this hour, but we managed to flag down one of them that took us to a university where we would be staying for what was left of the night. With the students on break, we would be using their dorm rooms while in Shanghai.

The next morning at breakfast, we learned that all the Bibles had been safely delivered, and we gave a collective sigh of relief. But not for long. Our mission had only begun. As was customary for our ministry group, we would go out each day, not knowing what to expect. We knew only that the Holy Spirit would lead us, and that's all we needed to know.

—

Catching a public bus to head into the city, we were herded by "Pushers," Chinese women in white coats who literally pushed as many people into the vehicle as possible until we were all packed inside like sardines.

When we got off the bus, we were met by a man named Pastor Moses—a wizened, old gentleman who had been imprisoned for his faith for twenty-three years. His emaciated frame spoke of starvation. At one time, he had boiled his leather belt to make some soup, thinking it would be his last meal. Another time, he had tried to commit suicide by sticking his finger into an electric outlet. But there was too little power to complete the deed. Yet, when he was finally freed and Christians offered to help him escape to a place where he could spend his last days in peace and safety, he refused. "I must share Jesus with my people," he said.

It was Pastor Moses who led us through the back streets of Shanghai, past ancient Chinese homes that hinted of former grandeur, to the home of another secret believer. This man had been a deacon in Watchman Nee's church.

Although he knew our language, he had not spoken English since 1948. Despite the fact that he had studied in the United States at the University of Michigan, he was not officially allowed to use his education to help his people. Nevertheless, he had secretly listened to James Dobson's teaching tapes on a gospel radio station and had translated the teachings into Mandarin to distribute to his fellow believers—all at the risk of his own freedom and possibly his very life.

———

Later that day after lunch, I walked alone into a park bordering the Yellow River to take in the beauty of the scenery, to pray, and to maybe witness to someone. We had been cautioned against doing anything to draw a crowd, so I simply gazed at the water. But I couldn't help saying aloud, "Beautiful! God made all this!"

An English-speaking Chinese man standing in a group of other nationals turned to look at me. "Oh, you believe in God?" he asked in a mocking tone. "Have you ever seen Him?"

"Have you ever seen love?" I retorted. "It's the same with God. You can't see Him, but the greatest exchange in history is our sin for His Son's righteousness."

"Ah, spotless," murmured a voice from somewhere nearby.

Some believer in Jesus Christ had been there before me, sowing good seed. *Thank You, Father.*

i

Interestingly, I learned that at some time in their history, it had become desirable for the Chinese to learn English as their ticket out of poverty. Consequently, there was a place in every community called the "English Corner," where you could always find someone who understood our language. Of course, our party made our way there frequently while in Shanghai.

Without fail, we were asked, "Why did you come to China?"

That was the question we were all waiting for, and the answer was quickly forthcoming: "Because God sent us here to tell anyone who would listen about the greatest gift He has ever given—salvation through His Son Jesus."

We always left gospel tracts with the people who gathered there. Once, we realized that a policeman had overheard our conversation, so we offered him a tract. He took it and began reading.

Please, Lord, lift the veil from his eyes, I prayed silently, *and from the eyes of those in every tribe, every nation, every tongue.*

———

In China, the only church allowed to operate publicly was government-controlled and was called the Three-Self Church, one of the largest Protestant organizations in the world. At the time of the writing of this book, it is estimated that the Chinese worshipping in the underground house church movement surpasses that number for a total of over 100 million believers.

While in Shanghai, we attended one of the Three-Self churches. After the service, an older woman approached me and invited me to go home with her. "Home" was quite a distance away, as it turned out, and this woman had to be in her eighties. But I could not refuse her since it was considered quite an honor for a westerner to be invited into a Chinese home. We walked all the way.

When we finally arrived, I found a house with large rooms but no furnishings. No doubt, in earlier days this had been an elegant dwelling, and this woman an aristocrat. But communism targets and punishes the wealthy.

We slept on quilts on the floor that night. And before I left the next morning, she gave me the best she had to offer—a plastic bag filled with sticks and leaves from a nearby field, her only source of tea. I left part of my heart with that dear woman that day.

Beijing Bound

Next stop was Beijing, the capital of China and the second-largest city. We traveled by train—a twenty-three-hour trip. The trip was not only long but also hard—hard seats, hard bed (six of us took turns sleeping, one hour each), but hardy souls. It was wonderful, as we were able to communicate with some of the Chinese people on board.

Had we been in the city to take in the sights, there were certainly amazing sites we could have seen. The Imperial Palace of the Ming and Qing dynasties. The Forbidden City, ancient home of Chinese emperors, composed of 980 buildings, lush gardens, and opulent temples, including the Temple of Heaven. Even though steeped in Buddhism, Taoism, and ancestor worship, these people had acknowledged the sovereign God of heaven; they just didn't know His name.

Tiananmen Square was the site of the student-led demonstrations protesting government corruption and standing for democracy, free speech, and free press. While civil unrest may well have been festering on my first trip to China in 1985, the massacre of innocent students and other civilians by Chinese armed troops would not take place until 1989.

Then, of course, there was the legendary Great Wall, spanning a total of over twelve thousand miles. History and travel books tell us that the Wall was built over the centuries for the purposes of defense, border control, regulation of trade, and immigration control. On my free day, I made the Wall my destination before returning to the hotel to do some last-minute shopping. My short walk on the Wall was not so impressive, but memorable. It was here I lost my traveler's checks—all $800 worth. I had saved the money to spend in Beijing, hoping to bring home some treasures to friends and family—at least some Cloisonné vases. Now I was broke.

That night, I dreamed that our bus driver brought the lost checks to me. And the very next morning at breakfast, one of our leaders announced, "The bus driver told me he found someone's traveler's checks. If that's you, see me after breakfast."

No real surprise here. As soon as possible, I shared my dream with our driver. Just another God-given opportunity to speak the message we had come all this way to deliver—that our God is real and that He loves and cares for His children.

———

That day, winds from the Gobi Desert kicked up, bringing swirling gusts of sand and an orange haze to make driving hazardous, not to mention blinding the eyes of the Chinese, many of whom depended upon bicycles as their only mode of transportation. In fact, we learned that sandstorms in this area were not uncommon. To combat the stinging sand, the bicyclists wore head coverings made of some kind of fine netting. With those unusual headdresses, they looked like a nation of beekeepers.

Home Again

No sooner had I arrived back in the States than I began to receive invitations to speak at schools and for women's groups, requests for interviews by reporters from the newspaper and radio, and opportunities to address church gatherings. Nobody knew much about China since it had been closed to outsiders for so many years. Therefore, the impact of this trip on my sphere of influence was huge. This school crossing guard became instantly "famous," highly favored rather than the object of scorn. In fact, one driver even pulled his car over to the curb and unloaded a case of wine from his trunk as a gift for me.

On my first trip to China, I had stepped into a whole new world. With growing insight into the suffering of persecuted saints in that faraway nation, the entire New Testament was validated for me. The book of Hebrews burst to life! It didn't cost me anything to love Jesus in America. It was costing these people everything.

There would be many more visits to China—twenty in all—before He gave Israel back to me.

Chapter 4

The Call Continues

"Have I not commanded you?
Be strong and of good courage;
do not be afraid, nor be dismayed,
for the LORD your God is with you
wherever you go."
Joshua 1:9

The trip to China in 1985 did indeed prove to be the first of many visits to that country. I was so moved by the stories I had heard and the example of those faithful saints a world away that I couldn't wait for the next mission opportunity to present itself. All I knew was that I was to keep my passport up to date and be ready. My constant prayer was, "Lord, I don't know where I'm going . . . or when . . . but I'm not settling for the American dream!"

When word of my travels reached one lady in our town, Sandy Whatley, she called me. "I have a heart for China too," she confided. "I'd love for you to go to China with me and take blankets to the Chinese pastors who have been imprisoned for their faith. I've heard that the prisons don't provide blankets for prisoners, and this is something I can do. Oh, and I'll pay your way."

Sandy went on to explain that she intended to make the blankets herself. Since silk can be printed on, she would print

Scriptures on plain white 8.5 x 11 silk sheets—verses from Psalms, Ephesians, Philippians. She would then sew the pieces together and insert them into a cotton pillowcase before covering it with brightly colored, patterned Polartec. She made ten of these blankets. She also wanted to take money to the pastors' families—if we could find some way to raise the funds. I had saved up only about $300 for China. We would have to pray about the rest.

You never know when God will show up, but this sounded like Him to me. On the other hand, when I mentioned it to Doug, he was not so sure. In fact, he was highly skeptical. "Honey, that's the craziest thing I ever heard," he sputtered. "Two women alone . . . taking illegal contraband into that country? What ministry is it anyway?"

"It's ChinaAid, Sandy said. Bob Fu out of Midland, Texas, heads it up. And we'd be with a tour group."

Doug: *I got on the phone right away and called the office of ChinaAid. A lady answered.*

"My wife and another woman want to go to China to take blankets to the Chinese pastors who are being held in prison," I explained. "Don't you think that's just about the craziest thing you've ever heard?"

"Yes, it is," she had to agree.

Then I had another thought. "On the other hand, my wife would go to the gates of hell to carry the gospel."

There was a long pause on the other end of the line. "Then . . . let's do it!"

But that wasn't the end of it, as far as I was concerned. Since Dabney barely knew this woman, I called to talk with her myself. Turns out she was a Southern Baptist who taught children in Vacation Bible School and held prayer meetings and Bible studies in her home. Dabney later learned that Sandy also had a tie to Lottie Moon, the famous missionary to China. So does Dabney. Her great-grandfather and Lottie Moon were second cousins.

And I knew that if two women started praying about something, God would provide. Sure enough, as word got out, they raised $10,000 for the Chinese pastors' families in thirty days.

We also learned that Bob Fu had been a student living in China at the time of the Tiananmen Square revolt and had been arrested and imprisoned before escaping to Hong Kong. Bob was in touch with the families of prisoners and arranged for us to meet up with them in Beijing.

No doubt this idea was of God. If not, I wanted no part of it. In fact, I never undertake a trip for the sake of another trip. It must be "unto" something *He* has planned.

Sandy and I booked a tour—a secular tour this time. We decided that we would act like the other tourists, but plan to meet with some of the pastors' family members to give them the money and blankets. Still, we would have to respect their dignity. The Chinese are honorable people and find it difficult to accept monetary help. So we assembled ten gift bags, each with a blanket and a red envelope containing the equivalent of $1,000 in cash. In their culture, red signifies honor.

When we arrived at the hotel in Beijing, at least sixty or seventy eager Chinese were waiting for us in the lobby. One or more of those who greeted us were pastors who had been released from prison. It was these men who told us about some videotaped testimonies they had recorded and asked if we might carry the tapes back to the United States to share with believers.

The pastors had brought the tapes with them, and we hid them in our hotel room. Though the police later came and searched our room, they never found the tapes. It was suggested that we wear them under our clothing. Once we had distributed the money, we put the tapes in the now empty money belts and wore them everywhere from that day on.

One of the older pastors asked if we would like to speak

at his church the following Sunday. We would have a Chinese interpreter, of course. He also invited us to visit the orphanage operated by his church. I was thrilled. But after a trip to Burma with Michal Ann Goll once, when we had ended up in an orphanage with nothing to give them, I had prayed, "Lord, don't ever let me visit another orphanage empty-handed."

That night, we made a trek on foot from our hotel across an interstate to the local Walmart—a three-story building with moving sidewalks. There we purchased gallons of oil, rice, soap, shoes, clothes, and flowers for the women. After our shopping spree, we hailed a taxi to take us and our load of supplies back to the hotel. Lacking a container to keep the flowers fresh, we stored them in the toilet overnight. Amazing how God helps us improvise.

The next day when we visited the orphanage with our treasures, the pastor went with us. He had secured a bus to take the children to a park for a picnic and to ride in little boats on the lake. Watching them enjoying this outing, the pastor said, "The last time I was in this park, I was led away in handcuffs to prison. I wanted to return in victory."

None of us would soon forget this excursion.

———

When we returned home to Franklin, Tennessee, we FedExed the videotapes to Bob to be used in an upcoming conference. No sooner had he received them than he called to invite me to speak at this conference. I was happy to share, although I did not consider myself a speaker. As they say, "God does not call the equipped; He equips the called."

At this conference, it was my privilege to meet Brother Yun, referred to as the "Heavenly Man" by many who noted his sacrificial lifestyle, enduring torture and prison time as he pioneered the Chinese house church movement. To my surprise, when we met, he grabbed me, hugged me, and said, "You are truly a mother in China."

High praise indeed—and so undeserved—from this man who had traveled the remote regions of China by bicycle as he shared the gospel with his countrymen under intense persecution.

Slow Boat to China

There would be many more trips to the Far East in the next few years. Some of them would be experienced with members of our church, other churches, the women whom I would mentor down the road, and sometimes, with Doug.

Doug: My first trip to China came a couple of years after Dabney's first. I knew the call on her life, but I had a bit of a struggle with the idea. I had no clue what role I could play on this mission. What did I have to offer? Maybe I could go this once and see for myself, especially since there would be some other couples from our church. I could always hang out with the guys.

It was neat too, having my own "travel agent." Dabney knew the drill—how to pack, what to pack, and, after arrival, when to speak, when to keep silent, and when to stand strong.

So here we were, on foreign soil. This time, the Chinese police were waiting for us in the customs office. They rounded us all up—except for Dabney and two of her friends, who ran out of the office with their luggage and down a side street, armed officers in hot pursuit.

But they didn't know my wife. When the police officers demanded at gunpoint that the women turn over their Bibles, Dabney politely refused. "I'm so sorry, but I cannot do that." She later told me that the Scripture that popped into her head was Acts 5:29: "We ought to obey God rather than men."

Going into the mission, we knew the risks we were taking. Anyone bringing in Bibles to this atheistic country could be imprisoned, or worse. We had heard the horror stories. But that didn't faze Dabney. To their surprise, one of the officers merely shrugged and said, "Then give me one." *He grabbed it and left without another word.*

Intimidation, met with fierce determination and faith. That's Dabney. That's our God.

As scary as it was to be caught by the Chinese police, I was glad. It allowed the rest of our party to get through customs without a hitch, taking the majority of the Bibles with them—except for Doug. They confiscated his Bibles too.

Doug: *Not on my watch! I was not about to sit back and allow that to happen. Later that night, I told Dwight Marable that I would go to Hong Kong and pick up more Bibles to replace those the local police had taken. I said, "Dwight, I didn't come all this way to twiddle my thumbs." Dabney insisted on going with me, of course.*

"Then take the night boat and load up with Bibles," Dwight said. "But be careful."

Talk about a "slow boat to China," but our adrenaline was pumping. In the dead of night, the guards at all checkpoints were sleepy and their posts were poorly lighted, so we slipped through without being interrogated. We made it to Hong Kong and back and delivered the Bibles to Dwight at the White Swan Hotel where we were staying.

So this was why I had tagged along? If so, mission accomplished.

Higher Ground

One trip to China was an unforgettable experience. Doug and some of the other men in the church were along for this one too, although we women had made it clear that intercession was our main purpose for going. Our goal on this prayer journey—to penetrate the border between China and Tibet, on the Tibetan Plateau, with the gospel.

Our destination on this particular day was a small village nestled high in the Himalayas, at fourteen thousand feet, where the first church in China had been established by Jesuit monks who had come up from Vietnam via the Mekong River. We would make our way by bus up a seldom-used and very steep and narrow road for the eight-hour trip, one way.

But before we embarked on the last leg of the journey, there was a small glitch—I was stricken with nausea and dizziness and was diagnosed with altitude sickness. I was so sick I had to be hospitalized and given IV fluids in both arms.

"Your wife . . . it kill her to go up mountain!" the Chinese doctor warned Doug. "She die!"

When I was finally in my right mind again, I thought, *If I die, it will ruin this trip.* There seemed no way I would be able to complete the mission—in the natural. But the Great Physician had another opinion. When I asked what He wanted me to do, He said, *Pack your Polartec!*

Acting on that inner prompting, I ripped out both IV lines, dressed in my warmest clothing, and, ignoring the Chinese doctor's warning, left the hospital. It was now about 3:00 a.m. The guard at his post was sleeping, and the gate was locked.

Looking over our shoulders, we could see the doctor who had attended me watching us through the window of my hospital room. She called down to wake the guard and instructed him to allow us to leave. Relieved, we walked through the now open gate, hailed a taxi, and went to the hotel. I showered, dressed, and packed my Polartec as the Lord had directed. By 6:00 a.m., we rejoined our group on the steps of the hotel, much to their amazement.

———

The challenges were far from over, however. The winding path up the mountain was so narrow it seemed to defy the ability of the bus driver to keep all four wheels on the road. With every turn, passengers on the right would lean left and vice versa. If we had gone over the side at any point, we would never have been heard from again.

Mike Pfieffer remembers this incident:

Mike: One time, a log from a tree felled by some loggers in the mountains above us shot across the road in front of the bus and plunged into the headwaters of the Mekong River below, forcing the driver to brake abruptly. He kept honking his horn, but the logs kept coming. Finally, the loggers heard him and stopped their operation long enough for us to get past. I'll have to admit, I was afraid for my wife and began to question if we should have come on this mission.

When we finally arrived at the tiny church, abandoned since the Communist takeover, it was locked. I was not only frustrated, I was also angry. These ladies had been determined to pray on-site, and we had come all this way across dangerous terrain to accomplish something for God. I pounded on the door and when no one came, I sank to my knees. "Lord, send someone to open up this church."

That was my prayer too. A young boy from the village took note of our dilemma and raced off, returning with a caretaker. Unfortunately, the caretaker spoke French. This is when we experienced another miracle. One of the ladies with us had gone on a mission trip years before and had learned a little French. She had not found it necessary to use her newly acquired language until this day. Recalling some phrases at that moment, she was able to communicate with him. Gratefully, we went in to pray and take communion together.

About that time, two women from the village appeared at the door of the church, and our French-speaking friend was able to invite them to take communion with us. "But where's the priest?" they wanted to know.

Doug, with his silver hair, was the most likely stand-in, so he led the service. The women wept as they took the elements. All those hours and all that danger—for two people. But it wasn't over.

Mike told us later, "Frankly, I had come along to provide guard rails for you women so you could do your own thing. Your relationship with the Holy Spirit is so much deeper. To be honest, I had never understood women and intercession until that day, but I wept right along with you."

The surprises continued. One of the women in our party removed an emerald and diamond ring from her finger and slid it onto the finger of one of the Chinese women. "So you will remember that what happened today was real," she told her.

Although the church had been abandoned for many years, the grapevines the monks had planted were still growing. After all this time, there was still life here.

This was never more evident than when Casey Long later testified:

Casey: A former missionary, Kim, was my roommate on this trip. She was hungry for the Holy Spirit, but she had not been baptized in Him. In fact, she assured me, "I'm a musician, and if God ever did that for me, it would have to be a sound I couldn't make up."

"Well, that wouldn't be a problem for Him," I told her.

We were standing in the cemetery of the church at the time with a lot of activity going on. Kim was ahead of me, when the Lord said to me, "Go and lay hands on Kim."

When I did, she fell out in the Spirit and this unusual sound—a kind of high-pitched, bird-like song—came forth. It went on for quite a while. I recognized it as a birthing-sound tongue.

When Kim finally caught her breath, she said, "Musically, I can't hit that note."

I nodded. "I understand."

"But you don't understand. It's physically impossible for me."

"God has given you your prayer language," I explained, and she began to bawl.

We will probably never know, this side of heaven, the full impact of this trip—or any other. We can only imagine that the

two village women—like the woman who met Jesus at the well—
went back home, eager to tell what had happened that day, with
a ring to prove it.

Whatever It Costs

In 2005, I learned even more about the true heart of Chinese
believers—the depth of their desperation and their desire to know
the Jesus they now loved despite the cost. We in the West know
little about the cost of discipleship with our comfortable Christianity, although the Bible clearly spells it out: "Whoever desires
to come after Me, let him deny himself and take up his cross and
follow Me. For whoever desires to save his life will lose it, but
whoever loses his life for My sake and the gospel's will save it"
(Mark 8:34–35). The truth is, I have always wanted *Him* more
than my comfort.

This trip to Shanghai would be a teaching trip to equip house
church leaders. And here they came from all over the country—150 young people—by bus, on bicycles, and even on foot,
knowing that they could be arrested, tortured, and even killed if
they were discovered attending such a controversial gathering.

Our group had commandeered a warehouse to show *The
Passion of the Christ* film in Mandarin Chinese. Meanwhile, the
young leaders willingly endured sleeping on a cement floor in
the warehouse for the privilege of viewing, for the first time,
this enactment of Jesus' death, burial, and resurrection. We wept
together, then took communion together, breaking the bread—
rice crackers—and pouring grape juice from teapots into tiny
little cups. Proof that this timeless memorial could be embraced
by any culture, at any time, anywhere.

To protect these precious brothers and sisters, we dressed in
typical Chinese attire. I even wore a black wig to disguise my
blond hair while teaching on deliverance. On our last Saturday
night in Shanghai—at midnight—everyone was outside, enjoying

the balmy evening air. Homes here were so tiny that their occupants seemed to burst from the doors. As a result, we had many observers for what would be a first for me—riding behind the driver of a motorcycle, a young man who oversaw several house churches. And so we rode, all the way from the warehouse to our apartment, my wig flapping in the stiff wind.

One More Time

In 2014, on what would be my final trip to China—until the Lord again opens the door—I traveled with a group from Grace Center School of Supernatural Living, along with some intercessors from Bethel Church, Redding. In our party were a dozen women, charged with the task of praying for missionaries from around the world who were now serving in China. These missionaries had been invited to a conference in Chengdu.

Chengdu is a teeming city located in the second-largest province in China and situated on a fertile plain, home to one of the largest agrarian populations in the world. With its abundant natural resources, which enable a thriving industrial and commercial economy, and its significant contributions to China's cultural history, ancient and modern, it is referred to as "Heaven on Earth." *An appropriate place for a gathering of believers*, I thought.

We had been warned that many of the missionaries were worn out, burned out, and on the verge of abandoning their calling. It would be important, therefore, for us as intercessors to speak life.

One of the first to present herself for prayer was an American woman I recognized from a previous trip. I had noticed her two teenage daughters hanging out with the adults and thought they looked rather forlorn. I determined to follow up with them if the opportunity presented itself.

The woman's story was tragic. As a young girl of eleven, she had been granted the gift of healing. When she was a teenager, her pastor, acknowledging this gift, asked her parents for permission to take her with him on visits to the sick. They agreed, and thus began a sordid tale of sexual molestation by this pastor.

When the truth came out, instead of supporting their daughter, her family blamed her for the abuse, and her father wrote her out of his will. As an adult, she married and, with a call still on her life, she and her husband went to China as missionaries. But even the missional group rejected her.

As a result, she had picked up a spirit of offense—against her parents, the other missionaries, and God. She was waiting for Him to validate her. When He did not, she became even more bitter and angry and virtually locked Him, along with the minister, her parents, and her colleagues into a mental prison cell. It was obvious that she would never be a joyful lover of the people she had come to serve until she used the key of forgiveness to unlock that cell.

Knowing we should never encourage missionaries to leave the mission field, I dared to address the root cause of her misery. "Go home," I urged her gently, "and make things right with your family. Then come back if the Lord leads."

A single tear slid down her cheek.

Intercessors don't always know what happens after their fervent prayers, and the woman and her daughters left, mingling with the crowd. After a few more days, the conference ended, and our group moved on to the next city.

There we met with an underground church of Chinese believers and some American ex-pats. One Sunday evening, I noticed a man eyeing me as if he somehow knew me. Eventually, he made his way over.

"Hello," he said. "You met my wife in Chengdu, and what you told her was exactly right. She reached out to her family and received a letter from them this week. She has been reinstated in the will and will inherit the house and property. We're going home."

Sending missionaries home is not always the desired outcome of our efforts, of course. But in this case, God's order needed to be observed. We must first restore communion with Him, then make peace with all who have offended us, forgiving them from the heart. Only then will we be able to give what we have received.

———

What you have heard about communist countries is all true. Communism itself is evil, wicked, and horrific—but the Chinese people are wonderful. They are my people. And my "one-time trip to China" became my calling.

Chapter 5

Rescuing Ling Ling

"Whoever receives one little child . . .
in My name receives Me."
Matthew 18:5

The next few years were filled with almost more items on my agenda than I could handle. I was still on the local board of Hadassah, volunteering in the Jewish thrift shop, and answering every "Go!" assignment the Holy Spirit prompted. High on my list, always, were those dear people half a world away who had become knitted into the very chambers of my heart, and I paid close attention to any news from both the Middle East and the Far East.

In 1989, there was the shocking report of an uprising in a city I had visited every year for the past three years—Beijing, China. The newscast detailing what had taken place on Tiananmen Square sent a shudder through my soul.

Tiananmen Square is named for one of the gates to the Forbidden City, located on the northern end of the 109-acre square. The name—Tiananmen—means "Gate of Heavenly Peace." We learned that every year, the emperor would make a sacrifice at this gate. "We know there is a God in heaven. We just don't know His name."

The name might mean "Gate of Heavenly Peace," but the place was anything but peaceful during the spring of that year. For weeks, Chinese students and other activists had demonstrated for political and economic reform, wishing to be free of overreaching government rule. Finally, in the late-night hours of June 3, military tanks and heavily armed soldiers advanced on the protestors, killing and injuring hundreds in a bloody massacre.

You might want to read the preceding paragraphs again because this information has been deleted from the Chinese history books. With tourism big business in China, "tour guide" is a coveted occupation. But I was shocked to hear one guide, who was supposed to know Chinese history, deny that this uprising ever took place.

When I questioned him about it, he asked in a sarcastic tone, "Were *you* there?"

China Call

Only a few months later, the Holy Spirit opened another door to that region, and a company of intercessors from our church, including Pastor Don Finto, were standing on the very flagstones where those deadly demonstrations had taken place. The stones were still stained with the blood of the young people who had died in their pursuit of freedom.

Don's personal testimony of his call to that experience is worth noting here. God moves in mysterious—and sometimes humorous—ways. We need to look and listen carefully, or we might miss His creative direction.

Don Finto: It was the clearest and most unmistakable call I have ever heard. And the last one I expected to hear.

A large number of us had gathered for our usual 5:00 a.m. prayer meeting to intercede for a group that would be traveling to China on mission when I heard myself praying, "And, Father, if You want me to go . . ." I stopped abruptly—mid-sentence. Had I really uttered those words? The truth is, I had absolutely no desire to go to China.

When that group dispersed at 6:00 a.m., I met with the administrative elders. Maybe they could bring some clarity to my dilemma. But I only heard, "Well, maybe you are *supposed to go."*

As it was still early after the meeting, I headed to a favorite bread company for coffee and a cinnamon bun. On the way, I noticed a billboard with a huge sign advertising a new restaurant in the area. The sign read CHINATOWN. But the last part of the name—TOWN—was blocked from my view by a building. So all I could see was the word CHINA!

Surely, the Lord wasn't writing in the "sky," was He?

I called my wife. Martha was the level-headed one. She'd tell me why I shouldn't go. But when I called, all I got in answer to my question was, "Do you think I should go with you?"

As it turned out, Martha didn't go. But I did.

It was a trip like none other. On Yom Kippur of that year, we took communion at Tiananmen Square, the scene of the bloodbath when government troops had fired on their own countrymen only months earlier. This was only one of several significant events that took place during that trip.

Another was the sense that a friend of ours, Sandra Womack, should fulfill a lifelong calling to the mission field—this mission field, China. But I wouldn't mention it to her until the Lord released me to share it with her.

As it turned out, no sooner had our group landed back in Nashville than we were greeted by a contingent of Belmont Church members to welcome us home—Sandra in the forefront. Before I could help myself, I blurted out, "Sandra, I believe you are to answer that call to missions. You need to go to China."

One year later, she was on her way . . .

. . . and I was in Hong Kong to greet Sandra, to help her find an apartment, and to stay with her for a couple of weeks until she became acclimated to her new surroundings. In addition, there was the tricky business of entering mainland China, crossing the border with "illegal materials." By now, I was an old hand at smuggling.

The others in our group, including Doug, were hesitant to leave me behind, but I was confident in the Lord. He who had been faithful to protect me as I attempted to accomplish His instructions to me, would be faithful still. Besides, there was a new development—and I was intrigued.

Crisis in Hong Kong

While Doug and I were in the ministry office in Hong Kong, only a few minutes before he and our group were to leave for the States, the phone rang. Since the two of us were the only people in the office at the time, Doug answered. It was Mickey Newman from the missions ministry office at our home church. She told us of a conversation she'd had with a gentleman who headed up an outreach on the campus of Vanderbilt University in our city, John Eaves. John had met and ministered to a Chinese medical doctor who was in our country to work toward his PhD in epidemiology, and John had led him to the Lord.

This Chinese doctor's story was heartbreaking. As a result of the government concern about the "brain drain" in China—the steady loss of highly educated citizens who were looking for better living conditions elsewhere—the law stated that Chinese people leaving the country temporarily must leave behind something of value. This man was forced to leave behind his wife and one-year-old daughter, Ling Ling.

The anxiety over his family had hindered his studies, and he was considering returning to China. The following year, his wife was able to join him, leaving their little daughter with his parents. The doctor's scientific research was significant. We later learned that he and his team were developing a cure for a childhood disease—RSV. Meanwhile, they were desperate to be reunited with Ling Ling.

John had contacted our church's missions secretary to request help for this family, and Mickey's answer had been instant and encouraging. "We have a team in Hong Kong right now who have been going in and out of China for two weeks. Maybe they can help find his little daughter."

When Doug heard this, his immediate response was, "Impossible! You've got to be kidding!"

At this, he handed the phone over to me. As I heard the message, the lion within me rose up, and the Holy Spirit began to download some items we would need. I heard myself barking out orders: "Please send, by FedEx, $2,000 for Ling Ling's plane ticket and all the paperwork Vandy has on this child and her family."

Now I understood. Despite the heated political climate, my further mission on this trip was to find Ling Ling somewhere in this vast country and reunite her with her parents in the United States. Knowing this, how could I possibly leave until she was found? Somebody had to try.

Home Away from Home

Once I had seen everyone off at the airport, I could turn my attention to Sandra. She had flown into Hong Kong with her nine-year-old son, John, and would serve as a missionary to this area.

The two of them were not exactly newcomers to this part of the world. Sandra and both her sons had made the trip to China in 1988, only two years earlier. The call she had received as a seventeen-year-old girl had been delayed while she married and had her children. With the death of her husband, she felt released to answer the call—and the Lord was allowing me to see its fulfillment.

What some still did not understand was my utter lack of fear in remaining behind to help our friend. By now, I was a pretty experienced traveler to the Far East. Often through trial and error and always with much prayer, I had learned to trust God with all of it—every twist and turn in the road, every step in His ever-evolving plan. In this case, I so wanted to witness Sandra, a woman of excellence, realizing her lifelong dream in serving God here in this ancient land.

We found a tiny apartment located near the northeastern border of Hong Kong and China in an area known as New Territories, or Shatin. Although there is much scenic beauty here—a winding river and lush parks, surrounded by verdant hills—this neighborhood might not make it to the top of a tourist's list of places to visit, unless it would be to tour the Monastery of 10,000 Buddhas. But we were no ordinary tourists. We were here on the King's business.

To accomplish this purpose, Sandra would need some supplies, including a microwave oven. Such items here were minuscule in comparison with those back home. In fact, when I first spotted the Chinese version of a washing machine, it looked like doll furniture—something a little girl might have in a playhouse. Still, whatever we purchased would have to be carried back to the apartment. Fortunately, it was only a fifteen-minute walk to a large, modern shopping center that included a train station for more distant destinations.

One of our first shopping trips was to pick up some items at the Asian equivalent of Walmart. Although Sandra would be needing the microwave and other heavier items, this time our objective was sheets and towels, along with a few groceries.

While the weather here is something like that of Florida—cold in winter and insufferably hot in the summer—there can also be the occasional typhoon. As we were making our way back to the apartment, our arms loaded with packages, one such cyclone struck. Fierce winds swept the streets, ripping the packages out of our hands. We were forced to chase them down, fighting to stay on our feet against the fury of the storm. Fortunately, nothing we had bought that day was breakable, and we arrived at our doorstep, drenched but delighted to be "home."

The papers from Vanderbilt had arrived the day after I had said goodbye to Doug and the mission team. When I was finally able to look through the paperwork, I discovered that most of it was in Chinese. Despite all my travels, I had failed to pick up enough of the language to be able to discover any clues to Ling Ling's whereabouts. What to do next?

The Hunt Begins

The obvious place to start was with the ministry that had sanctioned our group's activity in the region. Surely, they would know what steps we should take. But my inquiry was met with a stern warning: "Whatever you do, do not divulge any information about our name or our work here."

With that door closed, I considered checking with the U.S. Consulate in Hong Kong. Now down to one page in my passport book, I needed some additional pages and had planned to stop by to see them anyway. This time, though, it was the Lord who cautioned me, *Don't mention your search for Ling Ling. Let Me handle it.*

Careful to obey, I kept quiet about my plans when I visited the consulate office later that week to pick up the passport pages. But the clock was ticking, and I still didn't know where the little girl was. I had to content myself with the assurance that the Lord had things in His ever-capable hands.

———

One thing I knew—I had to make another run across the border with some Bibles, as I had done many times before. So, while Sandra and her son continued to get settled in, I prepared for a quick trip into Guangzhou, less than a couple of hours away by train.

Interestingly, some months earlier, I'd had two or three dreams that I was on a train in China, traveling alone. The dream was about to become reality.

Glory!

While en route, I ran into a couple of missionary friends who were traveling to meet with a man named Robert Morris. Morris was currently working to complete a translation of the Bible into the Lishu dialect, a project that had been underway since 1939. I was intrigued with the idea of meeting such a man—after delivering the Bibles to the drop-off location.

Meanwhile, I had brought all of Ling Ling's paperwork with me to Guangzhou, but the only thing I had been able to make out were several telephone numbers. Finding a bright red telephone booth at a market near our hotel (this was before cell phones, remember), I made some calls, hoping to find someone who could help me locate the child. But to my dismay, not a single person answered.

It was while visiting with Robert Morris that week with my missionary friends that a young man on a bicycle stopped by. Fortunately, the man, who introduced himself as "Adam," spoke English. As introductions were made and I learned that he often helped Morris, I felt prompted by the Holy Spirit to share my mission with him, and he offered to take a look at the papers I had brought with me.

As he scanned the paperwork, Adam's countenance brightened. "She in Shanghai with her grandparents. Her grandfather . . . a professor in the university there," he translated from the paperwork. Then, turning to me, he added, "In one week, I bring her *you!*"

At that moment, I had no idea of the impossibility of such a task. For one thing, I had brought no money with me, and Shanghai was 750 miles away. How could a boy on a bicycle begin to accomplish such a daunting task? For once, I was sorry that I was the type of person who simply took the next step without considering a strategy for accomplishing the end result. But the Lord had said, *Let Me take care of it.* And so I did.

In one week, I would meet Adam in the hotel where I had

been staying. Only this time, I prayed, he would have Ling Ling with him.

Meeting Ling Ling

Back in Hong Kong, I was faced with the exciting prospect of actually meeting the little girl at last. After helping Sandra with some housekeeping duties, I asked her to allow me a day to fast and pray. On Thursday of that week, I found the answer I needed. In 1 Kings 8, I read Solomon's prayer of dedication of the temple he had built in fulfillment of the promise God had made to his father, David. Several verses (41–43 AMP), seemingly specifically addressing my request, leaped from the page:

> Moreover, concerning a stranger who is not of your people Israel but comes from a far country, for the sake of Your name [and Your active presence]—For they will hear of Your great name [Your revelation of Yourself], Your strong hand, and outstretched arm—when he shall pray in [or toward] this house; Hear in heaven [Your dwelling place], and do according to all that the stranger asks of You, so that all peoples of the earth may know Your name [and Your revelation of Your presence] and fear and revere You.

This was my heart's desire. Not only to find a little girl and restore her to her family, but that "all peoples . . . may know [His] name and fear and revere [Him.]" His idea, not mine. As the Lord had been with David and Solomon, He was with me now and would not leave me throughout the final stages of this journey.

It occurred to me that I should pre-check my own luggage at the airport as I would have a child and her belongings with me when we boarded the plane. But how was I to win the trust of a three-year-old who had likely heard the Chinese proverb, "If you are bad, a white-haired foreign devil will come and eat you up!"

My hair was blond, but probably close enough to frighten a little one who had seen few Americans in her young life.

In the airport gift shop, I spotted a Chinese Cabbage Patch doll. Maybe that would do the trick to ease Ling Ling's first impression of me. I bought the doll.

———

The following Sunday morning, carrying only a small overnight case, I took the train to Guangzhou. After a cab ride to the hotel, I was in my room at 2:00 p.m. when the phone rang. It was Adam. "We here now . . . in lobby. You come."

I rushed to the lobby, holding the Cabbage Patch doll. There they were—the grandparents, an aunt with her little daughter, and Ling Ling, with her black hair cut short and dark, almond-shaped eyes gazing at me with intense interest. Then, to my astonishment, she spread her little arms wide and ran to me, exclaiming in Chinese, "I'm going to America!" Her family had prepared her well. From that moment on, her tiny hand was glued to mine.

For the next hour or so, the seven of us (including Adam, who stayed to translate) strolled the hotel gardens. On this walk with her family, I learned more about Ling Ling—her favorite foods, her bedtime routine, anything I might need to know during the short time she would be in my care. It was somewhat disturbing, though, that all her changes of clothing, toiletries, etc. were contained in one brown paper bag. Oh, well. I could supplement anything she might need before rejoining her parents in America—at the Chinese Walmart.

That evening, Ling Ling's grandparents rented the huge hotel dining room for our small group, and we dined on the traditional thirteen-course feast. It was a gesture of honor for this American who would be traveling at great risk, taking their precious grandchild to freedom.

Forty Long Hours

To my continued amazement, Ling Ling bonded with me immediately and came with me, rarely releasing my hand. Although her aunt accompanied us to the airport at 3:00 a.m. the next morning to make sure the child would be all right, Ling Ling adapted beautifully. But we had not anticipated the difficulty we would soon encounter from the airline officials.

For one thing, the guards eyed us with suspicion at seeing this blond American with a little Chinese girl. At first, they wouldn't let us proceed to the gate. Instead, we were escorted to a room filled with many desks, behind which were stationed airport personnel and military police. Juggling my carryon case and the brown paper bag with the child's possessions in one hand, and with Ling Ling still clinging to my other hand, I looked for the person who appeared to have the most authority. Spotting a white-haired gentleman, I approached and explained my situation.

Fortunately, he spoke English and understood my explanation. "So you are taking this child to her father?"

"Yes, sir, I am."

After what seemed an eternity, he stamped all my papers with red ink. Chop, chop! "You go now."

But this was only the beginning. Many procedures and many "chops" later, we were finally cleared to board the flight to Hong Kong. On board the plane, glances of distrust and outright disdain came from other passengers. Not a soul would even speak to me. With no adoption of Chinese children in those days, the threat of arrest was real should I be accused of kidnapping or taking a Chinese citizen out of the country without permission. I held my breath as police officers suddenly appeared, searching for someone, and released it only when they dragged two men down the aisle and off the plane.

In Hong Kong, the nightmare continued. At the United Airlines desk, a female official scanned the tickets I handed her and gave us a stern, appraising look, followed by a terse question. "What are you doing here? Your tickets were for yesterday's flight."

In the Chinese culture, it is a disgrace to lose face in a discussion—for either party. I knew the mistake was not mine, but I dared not mention that to this woman and jeopardize her position. Instead, Ling Ling and I stood at the counter for over an hour while the ticket agent checked and re-checked her files. Obviously befuddled, she apparently recognized her problem but did not know what to say to me. At long last, she handed us two boarding passes with no further comment.

Safely on board, I buckled our seatbelts for the long plane ride from China to Nashville—a total of forty hours. For most of the trip, Ling Ling slept or was content to nestle beside me.

Homeward Bound

When we landed in Seattle after the exhausting trans-oceanic flight, I discovered that our ordeal was not over. Now we had to pass U.S. Customs.

I handed the agent my huge yellow-and-blue folder filled with all the paperwork on Ling Ling. He rifled through the papers, looking puzzled. Then seeing one page, he beamed. "Oh, lady, *this* is all I needed." He seemed more relieved than I and quickly stamped the necessary papers just in time for us to make our connecting flight to Chicago before heading for Nashville.

I had wanted to call Doug while we were in Seattle and report on our progress, but there wasn't time. Meanwhile, he and the Lord were having a conversation, and I heard about it later when we deplaned in Chicago.

Doug: Oh, honey, I was in bed Sunday night, crying out to the Lord for your safety. I had called the United desk in Seattle, but they wouldn't give me any info on your flight at first. Weren't allowed to give anyone the names of people on the passenger manifest, he said. But when I told the guy your story, he relented and let me track your flight into Chicago.

Still didn't know if you had made the flight from Hong Kong, though. That's when I remembered something Paul Cain, a visiting prophetic speaker at Belmont, had said that day in church after his sermon. "There's someone named Dabney. I keep getting that name . . ." Following up after the service, I asked him what else he had heard, but he didn't have an answer. "Just got the name," he said.

I'll have to admit, I've been concerned. But Paul's word, then this one from Mark 16:20 gave me the assurance that God was hearing my prayers: "And they went out and preached everywhere, the Lord working with them." The Lord is with you, honey . . . but it can't happen until you go . . . and wherever He calls, you go.

When we landed in Nashville, exhausted but exhilarated, the whole place was abuzz with at least one hundred people from our church, carrying banners, balloons, and teddy bears. Ling Ling's mother and father were waiting at the end of the runway. At this point, with all bags and belongings checked, I was carrying the little girl and she was clinging to my neck for dear life as I prayed in tongues.

It appeared that Ling Ling had no intention of going to them willingly. After all, she had been left behind when she was barely a year old and didn't remember them.

I recalled what someone with expertise in such cases had advised. I should loosen Ling Ling's hold on my neck and give her to her parents without discussion, then simply back away and melt into the crowd. I was relieved that the large number of people at the airport would make my exit more bearable for her, and she wouldn't have to see me leave. It would now be necessary for her to become acquainted, all over again, with the couple who had given her life.

Glory!

The Rest of the Story

I didn't see Ling Ling again until her twelfth birthday, when I was invited to her home. Her mother shared with me that, for months, the child had begged to see me, calling me her "yellow-haired aunt." And they had set up many "pretend" phone calls to satisfy her.

Right away, Ling Ling took me to her room to catch up after all these years. I was pleased to see her report card with all A's and some artistic sketches she had drawn, then to hear her perform expertly on the violin. It touched me, too, to see the little Cabbage Patch doll I had given her, displayed prominently on her bed.

But it was a question she asked that gripped my heart. "Can you please tell me why my parents left me in China?" In the years since arriving in the United States, the girl had obviously wondered about this and had felt abandoned. No doubt she had never asked her parents since, in the Chinese culture, one is taught not to bring up unpleasant topics.

I took a deep breath before responding. "I'm sure they never realized that they wouldn't be going back to China to get you," I assured her.

There is a postscript to this story. Four years later, Doug was in Singapore and China. He had saved Adam's telephone number and gave him a call. They arranged to meet. To express our appreciation for all Adam had done in finding Ling Ling, Doug had brought along enough money for the young man to buy a brand-new bicycle. Since this is one of the main forms of transportation in China, Adam was elated. He couldn't have been happier if Doug had given him the keys to a BMW convertible.

Ling Ling's father did go on to receive his PhD and invited us to attend the presentation of his dissertation. He completed his research and now instructs other medical personnel around the world.

After high school and college, Ling Ling studied law, and with her law degree, she is now working as an attorney in the DC area.

As for me, I am simply waiting on my next assignment from the Lord while still praying for Ling Ling and her family. May He water the seeds that were planted in the heart of a three-year-old during those precious few hours.

Chapter 6

Company of Women

The Lord gives the command [to take Canaan];
The women who proclaim the good news
are a great host (army).
Psalm 68:11 AMP

Early in my walk with the Lord, He gave me a word—Psalm 68:11—a mandate that I have taken quite seriously. For one thing, I thought it more than coincidence that the address of Belmont Church, where we were members at the time, was 68 Music Square.

The more I pondered this verse of Scripture—in various translations—the more confused I became. It was not until I discovered the wording in the Amplified Version of the Bible that my heart leaped: "The *women* who proclaim the good news are a great host." To be sure I wasn't jumping to conclusions—that this was not merely the wording *I* preferred instead of *God's* intent—I sought the counsel of our Global Outreach leader, Mick Antanaitis. He assured me that this was, indeed, the most reliable translation.

Then, when a friend from the early days of my salvation came to the house to deliver the same word, I *knew*. What I was carrying was not just for me and my ministry. I was to mentor young women to live out and proclaim the good news for themselves and thus fulfill the prophetic purposes of God. In the next few years, I did not have to coerce or commission them. One by one, they came as I had come to Him—hungry for more.

As if in preparation for that time, Trish Mansfield and I decided to attend a conference in St. Louis. There were 3,500 crazy people ricocheting off the walls of a huge hotel that resembled King Arthur's Court. The instant we stepped inside, we felt the powerful Presence of the Holy Spirit pulsating through the conference room. One had to step over the bodies sprawled on the floor, out in the Spirit. It took Trish and me three days to get there, but at a definitive moment in time, we jumped over an imaginary line and said, "We're in, Lord. We say yes. We want all of You—whatever that looks like!"

———

A little later, while Doug and I were in a Christian bookstore in Franklin, Tennessee, speaking with a well-groomed, gray-haired pastor of a traditional church—you know the type—in came a couple who seemed to recognize us. When they walked over to greet us, I put out my hand. So did she. The minute our hands touched, we both slid to the floor in a rather ungraceful heap.

When we looked up at the pastor, his puzzled expression spoke volumes. *Can you two men not do anything with your wives?*

Doug and the woman's husband might have been wondering the same thing. But she and I knew. It was a Mary-and-Elizabeth moment for this woman—Sisse Pfieffer—and me. We were thinking, *Oh, what we could do for the Lord together! We're sisters!*

———

Over the years, between trips to China and other countries— sometimes with some of the younger ones—I have found myself nurturing the rising generation. And loving every minute of it. My eyes have seen the generation I have been waiting for, although

I didn't recognize it at first. Several other seasoned women of faith, including Sisse, would walk with me until the time came to launch into ministry to the young.

Many years later, I would hear negative reports about the so-called millennials, that they are "entitled, spoiled, self-centered," and I asked the Lord, "Are You going to pass this generation by?"

Not until the next morning did I receive my answer. But as is often the case, He began our interchange with a question to me: *Do you want to know what I call them?*

"Of course, Lord!"

I call them My "alabaster box people." They know that what I have put in them is holy, and they are not selling out for the American dream—houses, cars, careers. They are waiting tables, hosting, nannying other people's children, listening for My voice.

I knew this generation was going to be special. I had only to wait for the proper season. Meanwhile, the Lord had work for the older women to do—in China.

"Come and See!"

It would be a first, this mission trip to China with an all-female cast—six menopausal women and one twenty-something— Suzanne Stroud, Rachel Stroud, Lana Kantosky, Suzanne Young, Lynn Stefonic, Debbie Barry, and me. We had approached our pastor with what might have been perceived as an outrageous request in that day of "women, be silent in church." It was our desire to intercede on-site for Chinese women who were forced to abort their babies because of the one-child policy mandated by their government. There is something about actually traveling to a location and praying on the spot—but would we have the blessing of the church? To my surprise, the answer was a resounding "Yes!"

As I meditated on what had just taken place, I felt the Holy Spirit reminding me that every woman in Scripture has had to break protocol to do God's will—Hannah, Sarah, Esther, and so many others. So we would not be the first.

Earlier, I had received a touching invitation from a young university professor and his wife, Pete and Lauren Snyder, who were serving in a small village in Southwest China: "Will someone please come and see what God is doing here?"

No one had responded—until now. After the go-ahead from Pastor Steven, we made arrangements with Revival Church, an Asian outreach in Hong Kong, to take loads of Bibles into China under the radar, still a risky undertaking in 1996.

While our purpose was clear, the seven of us had already bonded in the Spirit to such an extent that our joy in being together for such an enterprise bubbled over. So much so that once we arrived in Hong Kong, Basil, our English-speaking guide from Singapore who would escort us throughout our trip, had cast many a doubtful glance in our direction on the flight to Guangzhou. He must have been thinking, *What can seven American women bring to the table?*

Once, he had asked, "Aren't you worried?"

"Should I be?" I replied.

"It's just that I have never seen smiling intercessors before."

We would disembark in Guangzhou and drop off the Bibles in duffel bags. Then we would continue on to Kunming before ending our trip in the city of Yuxi, home of our missionary friends.

On the way back to the airport from the drop-off site, to board the flight to Kunming, we noticed a basket of live snakes falling out of the truck ahead of our taxi, writhing and wriggling as they made their escape across the crowded street.

"Somebody's dinner," Basil explained, no doubt expecting us to react in horror.

Not a one of us flinched. But I could tell he was still not convinced.

That impression would soon change.

Miracle in the Golden Dragon

Kunming, China, with its mild climate, is called "The City of Eternal Spring." What a fitting phrase for the youthful exuberance we all felt. As far as we knew, no women had ever tackled such a task by themselves. We were giddy with excitement. No wonder Basil was skeptical of our motives as he observed us laughing and singing together.

We checked into the Golden Dragon Hotel, eager to discover what God was going to do through us in this place. The plan was to go to our rooms, freshen up and have dinner, then get a good night's sleep.

The next morning, we gathered for prayer in one of the hotel meeting rooms. For two hours, we prayed in tongues, interceding for the women of China, earnestly seeking God for our next move. I noticed that the youngest among us—Rachel, the daughter of Suzanne Stroud—was entering into this intercession with tears and fervent pleas, although I did not recognize her language.

At one point, her mother whispered to me, "But Rachel can't do that. She doesn't *have* a prayer language."

By this time, Basil was on the floor, sobbing. "I must ask your forgiveness," he said. "I judged you falsely. All this time, that young woman has been praying Jeremiah 31:15, 'A voice was heard in Ramah, lamentation and bitter weeping. Rachel weeping for her children, refusing to be comforted for her children, because they are no more!' And she has been praying—in Mandarin Chinese!"

Rachel later told us, "I felt I was interceding for the Chinese women who are forced to have abortions because of the government policy. At other times, though, I felt like I was preaching, proclaiming the gospel."

This—and Basil's tearful apology—was our first confirmation of women's mission trips. But there was more to come.

Invitation to a Feast

In the next day or two, we boarded a small bus, more like an extra-long Suburban in America, for the trip down the mountain. At the base of the mountain was our final destination—Yuxi— home of the couple who had invited us to this region, the reason we had made this pilgrimage in the first place. We had come to see what God was doing in Southwest China, and the Snyders were there to greet us.

On the first evening, we were asked to pray for a young man, Aaron Weaver, who was staying in their home and attending the university in that city. Aaron was hungry for Jesus, but he had never encountered the power of the Holy Spirit. After we prayed for him, the weight of God's glory was so heavy he couldn't move. It was the first time I had ever heard anyone say, "No, Lord, no more! I can't take any more!" By now, he was shaking and crying. We knew we were witnessing something holy and couldn't—or wouldn't—discuss it among ourselves. After that night, Aaron devoured the Word, and his life was radically changed.

Aaron's host, Pete, was a professor at the university. For some reason, Pete had fallen into disfavor with the administration. Weeping, he shared his story. And that is when I knew that a word from the Lord I had heard prior to this trip was about to be fulfilled. The Lord had clearly instructed me, *While you are in China, prepare a banquet and whosoever will, may come.*

While Pete's head was buried in his hands, I put my hand on his shoulder. "Would it help if you hosted a banquet and invited as many people as you wanted from the university, and served them whatever dishes you would like?" I asked.

He looked up, his face tearstained, but with an expression of hope and expectancy. "That would be awesome."

We rented a hotel dining room, placed an order for a thir- teen-course dinner—a typical Chinese banquet menu—and told Pete to invite the president of the university, the staff, the professors, and anyone else he chose. About forty dignitaries and others showed up for the event. In U.S. dollars, the total cost of this feast was only $75.

Following that evening, the breach between Pete and the university administration was healed, and he regained favor with the faculty. Which reminds me: We have a standing invitation to a feast with the King of kings. When we accept, we receive a royal pardon and the promise of favor and a rich inheritance. We can only hope and pray that our intercession for the Chinese people resulted in their acceptance to the feast of the Lord.

Love Story

On the night before our departure for the States, Rachel was sitting with Lauren Snyder on the sofa of their home when Lauren said to her, "I had a dream about you last night. In the dream, you were sitting with someone. Couldn't see who was with you, but there were two handkerchiefs on the floor in front of you. A handkerchief in a dream signifies servanthood. I believe you are to be a servant of the Lord."

Rachel smiled. "I had a dream too. I believe I am supposed to go home, quit my job, sell my car, and come back to China to homeschool your children so you can help your husband in the ministry."

Following through on this declaration, she was back in the country in less than six weeks. But I happened to know that Rachel did not have a heart for China until she said yes to God at that moment in Lauren's living room.

———

This was only the beginning of all that the Lord had in store for this young woman. A love story scripted by Hallmark or, better still, by the king in the book of Song of Solomon, began to play out.

On our trip, I had not failed to observe how much Aaron and Rachel resembled each other; they even dressed alike. Same hair and eye color; same jeans, sweaters, and boots. But they hadn't seemed to notice. While the Lord was molding them for His purposes, He had kept their focus on Him alone.

It wasn't until her return to China, while Aaron was showing Rachel the countryside, that the Holy Spirit opened his eyes. On a bridge spanning a lovely little stream, Aaron glanced over at Rachel. *This is your wife, son,* the Spirit of God whispered. For the first time, Aaron took note. *Lord, she's beautiful!*

Several months later, after Aaron received permission to court her, she said yes to his proposal of marriage, and they were married in July of that very year.

———

After they were married, Rachel and Aaron continued to live and serve in China for several years. Their first child was conceived there.

Rachel remembers being sick during the pregnancy and having to go to a dingy hospital and lie on a dirty examining table as the doctor listened for a heartbeat. Hearing nothing, he muttered, "No matter. No matter."

She wept again. For the child she was miscarrying. For all the aborted babies in China, and for all the mothers who would never hold them. If they disobeyed the law, Chinese people could lose their jobs, their homes. And before she was done, Rachel wept for this callous doctor and the abortionists in that country, speaking forgiveness for those who did not know the only One who has the authority to give life—or to take it away.

Rachel was a forerunner of all the young women who would cross my path and enter my heart in the years ahead. Everyone in this story—and those to come—said yes to the prompting of God's Spirit. We never know where our yeses will lead. Whether across the world or just next door. For Rachel and Aaron, their yeses brought them from China to Franklin, Tennessee, where they are associate pastors of a large suburban church.

There are huge yeses and small yeses, everyday yeses. Who knows what will come next when we say yes to God?

P.S.—Another Yes

I had met this Chinese lady in Kunming, that City of Eternal Spring. So, on her first visit to America, she was not prepared for our winters. Even in our Middle Tennessee town, it was unseasonably cold at seven degrees.

Over tea at Merridee's, a favorite local restaurant, we caught up with all the Lord was doing in our lives and the lives of those dear people I had ministered to back in China. So intriguing was our conversation that I almost missed the whisper. *Give her your coat.*

My friend and I rushed on, words tripping over one another as we attempted to fill in the gaps since our last encounter.

Give her your coat. The voice came again, a little more insistent this time.

We refilled our teacups and continue talking until….

Give her your coat. There was no mistaking it now. Holy Spirit intended to get my attention.

But, Lord, I like *this coat. It's my favorite rabbit coat—and it's freezing outside!* I pushed aside the ridiculous argument, took off my coat, and draped it around her shoulders.

Shaking her head, she said, "No, no! I could never accept such a magnificent gift!" And she removed the wrap and handed it back to me.

Twice more we repeated this ritual, but after the third attempt to return my coat—the honorable thing to do by her code of ethics—she accepted it and snuggled into its warmth gratefully.

After tea, we said out goodbyes, and she left with another friend. I hopped in my car, turned on the heater full blast, and hurried home, only a few blocks away.

But that's not the end of the story. The Lord wasn't through teaching me. A short time later, He lavished upon me three mink coats, one mink vest and a mink hat! In God's economy, His gifts are far more generous than ours!

Chapter 7

The Glory Girls

And the Word became flesh and dwelt among us,
and we beheld His glory, the glory as of
the only begotten of the Father,
full of grace and truth.
John 1:14

A little bit of flour by itself does not make a delicious pie. But add some sugar, a little butter or shortening, and the filling of your choice, and you can bake up a tasty dessert to serve your family.

By ourselves, we're not enough. But together, once we have grasped the power and glory of God resident within us as true believers, we make up the ingredients to satisfy a hungry soul. Not only that, but with the anointing of the Holy Spirit, we compose a force to send the enemy packing.

All of us—a group of women who were members of Belmont Church at the time—had experienced the initial infilling of God's Holy Spirit and, as time passed, additional manifestations of His Presence. But we wanted more. Having heard about an unprecedented outpouring that was taking place in Pensacola, Florida, at the Brownsville Assembly of God Church beginning in 1995, several of us were determined to see for ourselves, and the following year, we made plans to travel to the Sunshine state.

Glory!

Pensacola Pentecost

The revival, which would continue for six years, was already attracting people from around the world. Two and a half years of prayer on the part of Pastor John Kilpatrick and many saints had preceded this work of God, and we had come to receive the fruit of their intercession.

Each of us was impacted powerfully during our time in Pensacola. While few words could begin to express all that the Holy Spirit was doing in us, Casey Long shares her experience with eloquence—and a bit of wry humor.

Casey: I have the imprint of Dabney's foot on my backside. When word came of this invitation to go to Pensacola, she pointed her finger at me and said, "You'd better go!" I went, along with about ten of our Belmont sisters. When God—and Dabney—call, it's best to say "Yes!"

How do you express the inexpressible? God's magnificent Presence . . . angelic visitations . . . a vision of heaven . . .

As we worshipped—the most glorious worship ever—I felt the fire of God like an immediate physical burning, loving me, purifying me. I was worshipping with my hands up and couldn't put them down as the weight of His glory consumed me, beginning with my toes and moving up my body to my head.

As the worship progressed, I found myself leaning backward, arms still outstretched, until my head hit the back of the pew. "I don't want You to stop, Lord," I prayed. "But this is really uncomfortable."

It was then I felt someone cushioning my head with their hand.

After the service, I turned around to see who had been so thoughtful. "Thank you for putting your hand under my head," I said to the lady immediately behind me.

"Oh, it wasn't me," she said. "The Lord clearly told me, 'Don't touch her.'"

"But someone . . ."

Why should I have been surprised? It was a weekend of supernatural occurrences, each one surpassing the one before. I am forever changed!

Each of us could try to explain what happened that weekend as the Holy Spirit moved sovereignly among us, gifting us with His Presence in creative ways. So much so that we returned many times in the next few years, soaking in the precious Presence.

Hungry for even more, we were always alert to new opportunities to receive and then to share what we had experienced.

Sunderland—Spiritual "Wonder-land"

In 1999, as word spread that Sisse Pfieffer and I were planning a trip to Sunderland, England, the site of a profound outpouring of the Holy Spirit in the early 1900s, and again in 1995, a dozen women had signed up before we knew it. Only one elected to stay behind to pray for us after writing personalized notes and Scripture verses for each day we would be away.

In preparation for the trip, we read a book by Norman Grubb entitled *Rees Howells: Intercessor.* This book was a breathtaking read. How the intercession of one man from Wales, willing to die to self and empowered by the Holy Spirit, affected not only the people around him but ultimately the outcome of a world war. We might never attain the intercessory power of Rees Howells, but we knew his Source. The same Spirit is within *us.*

There was divine purpose in our journey, not some wild-haired scheme hatched up by a dozen crazy women. We couldn't wait to discover all that the Holy Spirit had in store.

———

Sunderland is a port town in the northeastern part of England, bordering the North Sea, not far from Scotland. We were told that in the mid-1800s, this town was the largest shipbuilding center in the world. But that was long ago, and the place has since lost some of its luster. Still, it was everything—and more—we could have asked for. Our purpose was, again, neither sightseeing nor shopping, but prayer and enjoying the Presence of the Lord here where so many storied saints had gone before us.

As early as AD 300, some monks in simple burlap robes left the grandeur of Rome to travel to Northumbria to wash the feet of the godless Celts living there. Much later, in the 600s, Brother Cuthbert served this area, spreading the gospel wherever he went and performing miracles of healing and casting out demons much like the biblical apostles. His chief delight, though, was enjoying the Presence of God, and in his latter years, he retreated to Holy Island, or Lindisfarne, off the coast of North East England. Here, he prayed by the hour and often sought God in the frigid waters of the North Sea. Legend has it that the Lord supernaturally kept Cuthbert warm while he was interceding and sent an eagle to catch fish for him to eat.

We had been told that there was still such an aura of the divine there, and we wanted to visit and pray on-site. Only one problem. The Lindisfarne Causeway, connecting the island with the coast, is submerged in seawater twice a day, and we had to choose our visitation time according to the tides. Fortunately, the bus driver for our stay in England, John, a big, amiable guy, offered to drive us across, and we spent one whole day on the island. The very soil is saturated with the prayers of the saints, and we added our own, praying over the generations—past, present, and future.

I had a very personal reason to be in this location. As a descendant of one who had fought with William the Conqueror, invading the area with his barbaric men, raping and pillaging, I felt a heavy burden of responsibility for my ancestor's actions.

Walking the beach, I prayed Daniel 9 with humility and tears:

> O LORD, great and awesome God, who keeps His cov-
> enant and mercy with those who love Him, and with

those who keep His commandments, we have sinned and committed iniquity, we have done wickedly and rebelled, even by departing from your precepts and Your judgments. . . . O LORD, to us belongs shame of face, to our kings, our princes, and our fathers, because we have sinned against You. . . . O LORD, hear! O LORD, forgive! O LORD, listen and act! Do not delay for Your own sake, my God! (vv. 4–5, 8, 19).

With these ancient words, I felt the weight of generational guilt lift from my spirit.

Golden Dust from the Streets of Heaven

Our original intent in visiting this part of the British Isles was to attend a prophetic conference in the home of what had seen the birth of the Pentecostal movement in England. All Saints Parish Church could not contain all the attendees who had registered, so the conference coordinator had rented a larger facility.

We were thrilled to be here, expecting great things in this land of spiritual giants. One woman from the church in Sunderland had actually sat on the lap of Smith Wigglesworth when she was a child, and another gentleman had served with him in ministry. And we sensed that the legacies of such spiritual fathers as John Knox and John Wesley were almost palpable in the very atmosphere.

Three of the conference leaders were people we knew: James Goll and Cindy Jacobs, generals of the prophetic and of intercession, along with Brenda Kilpatrick, wife of the pastor of the Brownsville Church (although Brenda never made it to the platform; she was prostrate on the floor at the altar the entire time). Since they also recognized us, at the very last minute we were asked to open the conference with a procession of flags. The problem was we didn't know what we were doing. That is, except for a couple of us—Sisse Pfieffer had brought along some flags, and Barbara Robinson offered to tutor us in the art of using flags in worship.

"Oh, no!" we had groaned.

"Oh, no problem!" they assured us.

Fortunately, with Barbara to coach us, we had a little time to learn the procedure before the first service, and we were given an overflow room in which to practice. With eleven of us and three aisles in the main auditorium of the conference center, we would break up in groups of three and four. Alternating with flags and lighted candles in shallow bowls filled with frankincense—one woman with a flag, the next with candle and bowl lifted high—we would process down the aisles, then flank the podium. If all went well, it would work. Barbara assured us that it would be a piece of cake. Easy for her to say; she was a worship dancer and had taught liturgical dance all over the world.

It was Barbara's husband, Mickey Robinson, founder of Prophetic Destiny International, who was leading a class once when I experienced another encounter with God. I found myself weeping uncontrollably—not because I was sad but because something was opening inside of me. As the tears flowed, I could feel a shift. It was transactional—an emptying of self so the love of God could pour through me to others.

We were about to experience another such moment. However, an additional unknown was our cue. We were to listen for a certain worship song before proceeding down the aisles, but since we didn't recognize the music or know the worship leaders, this, too, was questionable. Oh, well. We would let the Spirit lead. He knew all the cues.

As we were practicing in the overflow room, we noticed something unusual. There were golden flecks all over the black Naugahyde chairs. "Look at you!" someone said, brushing some flecks from my shoulder. "There is golden dust everywhere."

After leaving the overflow room, we assembled at the back

of the auditorium. As others entered to take their seats, we could hear their shocked outcries: "What is that shiny golden stuff? The horses in heaven must be pawing the streets."

I can assure you, we had never prayed any more fervently. In answer to our prayers, the Holy Spirit led and we followed. In perfect symmetry and pacing, each of us carried our flags and lifted our lighted candles, the scented smoke rising to signal the arrival of God's Spirit to anoint this gathering. What could have been a disaster turned out to be a fitting prelude to what was an amazing session. James spoke on Israel, an important message that had not yet been delivered at that time. It was he who later dubbed us "the Glory Girls."

Upon leaving the conference center after the service, we headed for the bus where our driver was waiting. Still reeling from the heavy weight of our encounter with the Holy Spirit, we stumbled forward. Thinking we must be doing a lot of drinking in those meetings, John met us with a big grin and a large bottle of wine.

"Oh, it isn't what you think, John," I tried to explain. "We aren't drunk. This is the Holy Spirit. We're just feeling His loving nearness."

We were not only enjoying His Presence, He was also knitting our hearts together. Back at the hotel, we lingered in the lobby to fellowship with many of the people from other nations who had come to attend this event. While some onlookers remained in the bar area, drinking their beer, others sought us out for prayer. Over these few days, beautiful new relationships were formed that would last a lifetime…and beyond.

Holy Ground

The next day, a young man who had observed our enthusiastic embrace of this land and its spiritual history approached us. "Good morning, ladies. My name is Peter. Would you like to see

Glory!

where Smith Wigglesworth was baptized in the Holy Spirit?"

Would we?!

From some research I had done, I already knew that Mr. Wigglesworth, one of the pioneers of the Pentecostal movement in England, was born to a very poor family in Yorkshire. Because he had to work in the fields and later, in a factory, to help support his family, he had no formal education. In fact, when he married, it was his new wife, a former Salvation Army preacher, who taught him how to read his Bible. He had been saved at an early age and baptized by immersion, yet he felt that something was missing….

During the great Sunderland revival of 1907, Smith visited All Saints Parish Church where Bishop Alexander Boddy was preaching. Hearing that the presence of the Holy Spirit was so strong in these meetings that many were being healed and filled with the Spirit, Smith decided not to wait until the evening service, but went to the parsonage next door to the church. The bishop's wife, Mary Boddy, answered his knock.

"Can you help me?" Smith asked. "I want to receive the baptism of the Holy Spirit."

"Then come around to the kitchen door, and I will pray for you," she replied.

And that is exactly what happened. In the bishop's kitchen, after Mrs. Boddy's prayer and laying on of hands, Smith was filled to overflowing with the Spirit and began to speak in a language he had never heard before.

Not long afterward, he was asked to preach in that very church, a small congregation at the time. So anointed was he that at least fifty souls were saved that day.

Eager to visit those sacred spots, my friends and I followed Peter to the parsonage, a nice, brick house that was boarded up with plywood. A FOR SALE sign was posted in the yard. The current occupants of the church must not realize that they would be selling their inheritance.

In awe, we walked around, soaking in the Spirit-charged atmosphere. The Presence of God was still strong in this place. So strong that none of us could stand, and we landed on the ground in a tangle of arms and legs. We were almost seasick from shaking. Caught up in the exhilaration of the moment, we began singing, then laughing. Jesus was there with us.

About that time, the warden of the church (something like a church administrator) drove up. Noticing our group in this undignified state, he got out of his car and stepped up to speak to us. "Perhaps you would like a brief tour of the church," he suggested. "Some ladies have gathered there for choir practice, but they won't mind waiting while you have a look-see."

"We would love to!" we agreed, scrambling to our feet to accompany him to the churchyard next door. Ancient trees presided over the landscape, and wildflowers bloomed bravely against a stone wall to the rear of the building.

The old brick church was small but lovely, and its arched doors swung wide and welcoming. The moment we crossed the threshold, moved by the enormity of what had taken place here, Cindi Whitman began to sing:

We are standing on holy ground,
And I know that there are angels all around.
Let us praise Jesus now.
We are standing in His presence on holy ground.

To our left near the front of the sanctuary was one of those crow's nest pulpits where both Boddy and Wigglesworth had preached. Casey wanted to go up there, but soon after stepping behind the pulpit, she disappeared from view.

"At first, I just leaned over to take off my shoes," she explained later. "Smith Wigglesworth is my hero. I was thrilled to be in the place where he had preached and led so many to Christ. I was telling the Lord how cool it was, what a gift it was to be there when I felt something like a God ball hit my head—hard! I couldn't stand up. I was moaning and groaning loud in my spirit. That's when I started worshipping."

As if the tour of the church was not enough, the warden then invited us to return to the parsonage, where he had a key and could let us in. In a holy hush, we moved from room to room, ending in the very kitchen where Smith had been baptized in the Holy Spirit. The perfect "amen" to our trip.

But the Lord had one more surprise for us, confirming the suspicion that He truly has a sense of humor. As we were boarding the bus to return to our hotel, the warden ran after us. "Ladies, ladies! A moment, please!"

Thinking maybe one of us had left something behind, we turned to hear what he had to say.

Panting with exertion, he paused to catch his breath, then spoke. "A passerby noticed your . . . um . . . predicament a bit earlier and reported to the constable that 'some ladies are throwin' themselves about in heaps in the front yard of the parsonage!'

"When the constable heard that—and not for the first time, I might add—he simply said, 'Ahh . . . not to worry. It's Pentecost Sunday, the feast day of John and Charles Wesley. God must have wanted Himself a pah-ty!'"

Dreams and Visions

Since we were so near the Scottish border, a stop in Scotland was definitely in order. Oddly enough, one of the most memorable parts of our visit to Edinburgh occurred for a member of our group one night in the hotel where we were staying.

Carol Goodwin shares this story:

Carol: Early in the morning around 4:00 a.m., I woke up, startled by the sense of a presence in my room. I didn't open my eyes but pulled the blanket over my head and curled up in a fetal position. I was petrified. Not because I felt something evil nearby. Just the opposite. I felt the Presence of holy God.

While I was under the covers, I had the mental image of a ticker tape, listing every wrong thing I had ever done. As I read each misdeed, I could only pray, "I'm sorry! I'm sorry!" It was the Light of His holiness exposing the darkness of my heart. I even tried to wake my two roommates, but neither of them stirred.

Then I had a vision of John Knox's church. Don't know how I knew it was his church, but I knew. After that, I saw a picture of a woman, and heard the name "Maria" and a time—one o'clock. This was the first time I had experienced a vision with this much detail, and I welcomed the adventure with anticipation.

The next day, I was eager to visit the John Knox church to see if we could find the woman in my vision. We arrived promptly at one o'clock—when a service was underway—but there was no sign inside of anyone resembling the woman I had seen.

When we stepped outside after the service, there she was! She was sitting on a bench, talking with another woman. With all this so new, I wasn't quite sure what to do, but felt compelled to walk over and speak to her. When I asked her name, however, it was not Maria. Disappointed that every aspect of my vision was not lining up, I didn't wait around to find out more and returned to the hotel.

In my room, I dissolved into tears, heartbroken that I had not pushed through in faith when the circumstances shifted a bit. I felt like such a failure. Later, the Lord told me that He would not give me visions for a while until I could move out in obedience, trusting Him for each part of the journey even when I don't have clear direction as to the next step. That's what faith is all about—leaping into the unknown, yet knowing His Spirit is there ahead of me. I tell myself that now I will obey, no matter how foolish or scared I feel.

Carol was no newcomer to the things of God when we made that trip. She was born again, water-baptized, and filled with the

Spirit. In addition, she and her husband, Myron, had served as missionaries to Africa for fifteen years. Apparently, the Lord simply wanted to give her even more of Himself.

After that divine encounter in Scotland, Carol and Myron became mission pastors for the best-equipping church in the region. And God again began giving Carol dreams and visions that have proven to be spot on. In fact, observing her minister is like watching an action-packed movie. The impact of that mission trip years ago lives on in all the many lives she touches.

The Humorous and the Holy

We had rented a bus for the two weeks of our stay in Northern England and Scotland and, when the conference was over, we still had some time left. Filled with the inexpressible joy of the Lord, we didn't want the experience to end and invited our main speaker, James Goll, along with his entire family—wife Michal Ann, their four children, and even their nanny—to join our party of women. There was room for all in the bus.

In Edinburgh, we spent one glorious evening together in my hotel room, reliving the event and the friendships we had made. There was lots of laughter, as James is a consummate comedian, along with having gifts of prophecy, teaching, writing, ad infinitum.

———

After returning from our visit to Sunderland and being newly inspired to spread the gospel of Jesus Christ, yet still feeling grossly inadequate, I ran across this quote by Smith Wigglesworth:

> We must be edified before we can edify the church. I cannot estimate what I, personally, owe to the Holy Ghost method of spiritual edification. I am here before you as one of the biggest conundrums in the world. There never was a weaker man on the platform. Language? None. Inability— full of it. All natural things in my life point exactly opposite

to my being able to stand on the platform and preach the gospel. The secret is that the Holy Ghost came and brought this wonderful edification of the Spirit. I had been reading this word continually as well as I could, but the Holy Ghost came and took hold of it, for the Holy Ghost is the breath of it, and He illuminated it to me.[4]

These words could have been written to describe *me*—or, at least, my perception of myself. Yet, "the Holy Ghost is the breath of it." Smith Wigglesworth may have spoken those words, but it is my own personal credo. The Spirit of the Living God is my life. He is my breath. He took hold of me.

Alone, I am not much. But together, with my sisters and the anointing of the Holy Spirit, I can go places where God has been before and invite Him to revisit the ancient wells.

The Deborah Ring

Had Michal Ann Goll, James Goll's beloved wife, not rushed off to heaven so soon, she would doubtless have been the original "Glory Girl." In her brief lifetime, Michal Ann accomplished more for our Lord than most women in a full lifespan. So, when Cindy Jacobs, founder of Generals of Intercession, decided to appoint twenty women as part of a Deborah Company of prophetic intercessors, it was no surprise that Michal Ann was among the Deborahs chosen.

As a surprise gift for her, James ordered a Deborah Company ring commissioned by Cindy for her generals. The gold ring was designed with a black onyx center stone, set with diamonds and flanked by two bumblebees symbolizing intercession. I was shocked to learn that, in her will, Michal Ann had left her Deborah Company ring to me!

In my heart, however, I knew this ring was not mine to keep. The Lord would show me the rightful owner in time….

Several years later, in Birmingham, Alabama, while at a

conference where Cindy Jacobs and James Goll were speaking, I wore the ring in memory of Michal Ann.

The audience was composed of both white registrants and a large number of African Americans. Suddenly, Cindy focused on one elderly black woman, seated near the front, and began to prophesy over her. This extremely intelligent woman, a native of Mobile, had marched with Dr. Martin Luther King as a child and had often ridden in the back of the bus with her grandmother. It was her deep desire to attend medical school to become a doctor. But no white school would accept her in those days.

In fact, the governor of her state, George Wallace, an outspoken racist, was shot during a political speech advocating "segregation forever."

Ironically, by this time the woman had received her medical degree from Tuskegee University and was one of the doctors attending him when he was hospitalized for the gunshot wound that left him permanently paralyzed.

"Governor Wallace, I cursed you for what you said and did to my people," she confessed. "But my calling is to heal, not hurt, and you are my patient. And I forgive you."

I knew instantly that this courageous woman was to receive the ring. Stepping to the side of the platform, I motioned to Cindy and whispered to her what the Lord had prompted me to do. She then insisted I share with the audience the story of the ring and why this woman should have it.

I don't recall exactly what I said that day, but afterward, Cindy came to me with an expression of wonder on her face. "Dabney, you don't know what you've done today! You don't know what you've done!"

Apparently, in that culture, what affects one affects all. When this doctor received the ring, all of her sisters in that room received the ring. It was a God-moment, and He was glorified!

Chapter 8

Into All the World

*"Go therefore and make disciples of all the nations
[help the people to learn of Me, believe in Me,
and obey My words], baptizing them in the name of
the Father and of the Son and of the Holy Spirit."*
Matthew 28:19–20 AMP

The river was flowing, and I wanted nothing more than to be in the middle of the stream. So when the invitation came for a prayer and fact-finding mission to Northern Iraq, also known as Kurdistan, I was all in.

Despite the intense conflict raging in the Middle East, many in that region were coming to know Jesus as their Savior, including an Iraqi man. Yousif was a geologist by training and a missile radar technician in Saddam Hussein's army. Having given his life to Jesus in an encounter in Baghdad, Yousif and his wife, Alia, a physicist who managed an industrial factory, together with their three small children, moved to Northern Iraq to lead Bible studies for the Kurdish people. This man had seen the need for a church, yet there was no pastor, and our team had learned about their need.

On this trip, only two women—Marilyn Layton and I—joined a team of eight men who were elders from Belmont and others from the community of faith, including a medical doctor. Upon arrival, we found the landscape in that part of the world littered with reminders of endless wars, from centuries past to the present-day conflict. Towns in shambles. Bombed-out buildings. Streets destroyed. And in more recent years, mass graves, marking the genocidal massacre committed by a terrorist who had risen to power, Saddam Hussein. His troops were still bombing.

Yet, in one walkabout, we stumbled across the remains of a synagogue, a star of David emblazoned across an arched door that was still standing. We took that as a sign that God was reminding His people that He had not deserted them. In truth, because of the faith of the Kurdish Christians and Jews in this area, hope had continued to rise from the rubble. We were here to encourage and reinforce that faith as well as to find a pastor for the embryonic church.

Rooftop Reverie

From our vantage point in the area where we were staying— sequestered in a fortress-like house—we could see American and Iraqi fighter planes flying toward each other, then banking away without engaging. Tension was mounting, and to make matters worse, because of damaged infrastructure that had not yet been repaired, we had been without running water for three days.

When the time came for a meeting with Yousif, the discussion focused on the problem of finding a Christian pastor in a land where the Chaldean Catholic Church, Assyrian Orthodox Church, and Islam, were predominant. In this war-ravaged country, the atmosphere was ripe for the gospel of the One True and Living God.

I couldn't help thinking that the answer seemed simple enough. Our church at home was an apostolic church and could legally ordain Yousif as pastor. Our men were batting ideas about. Maybe one of them would get around to the solution eventually. Still, respecting the Middle Eastern culture, which holds that women keep silent in the presence of men, I said nothing. *Not much different from "women, keep silent in the church" back home,*

I thought. And that led me to some somber introspection. I had found that it is difficult to remain silent under authority when those in authority aren't sure what to do.

I recalled that a dear friend and prophetic intercessor once stepped "out of line" and prophesied in a public service. Someone "in authority" later told her in a back room never to do that again. She complied at the time, but several years later, I called her out on it. She was a forerunner of a powerful ministry God had in mind for her. It's dangerous to be a forerunner. Just ask John the Baptist. It can cost you your head! The goal is not to be offended.

She wasn't the only one who'd had to wrestle with an offense. I once got my own feelings hurt at church. Where else? Doug wasn't affected, but he was hurt for me. I wrestled with that thing all night and into the next morning.

Finally, the Lord said to me, *You've bloodied your toes on this stumbling block, but you have a choice. You can continue to bloody your toes, or you can cast it into the sea and have something to stand on when you need to walk on water.*

At the time, I had no idea that I would be tested—in Northern Iraq, of all places.

—

A little later, with a political visitor expected, Marilyn and I were asked to leave the room and go up to the roof while the men greeted their guest and continued to talk. On the way upstairs, I muttered, "Really, Lord? All this . . . and three days without a shower?"

Suddenly, the whole thing—the ongoing conflict, the bombings, the planes flying overhead, the indecisiveness of the men, and finally, being dismissed from the conversation like disobedient children, dirty ones at that—seemed absurd. I started laughing and couldn't stop. Here we were on a rooftop in the Middle East, like Bathsheba in the Bible. At least, Bathsheba was taking a bath!

Unexpectedly, the joy of the Lord filled me to overflowing, and Marilyn joined in. The sound carried everywhere, and many people out on their roofs couldn't help overhearing. I believe the Holy Spirit laughter spread from rooftop to rooftop, breaking off the heaviness and gloom that enveloped the area.

———

When the visitor left, Marilyn and I were invited back into the conversation, and I decided to take a chance and mention my suggestion.

"Great idea," they agreed, and one by one the men picked up the ball.

"We could rent a hall for the ordination service . . . and hire security," said one of them.

"Yes, and I could easily print off a certificate of ordination from the internet," added another. "There has to be a frame around here somewhere."

Almost overnight, the plans were made and executed. After receiving a final blessing from the body of elders at home, we welcomed seven hundred people, who crowded into the hall to see Yousif ordained as pastor of the first non-denominational Christian church in Northern Iraq. After we had poured oil over his head, much like Aaron in the Bible, the newly anointed Pastor Yousif took several young people from his Bible study to a nearby river. There, in those beautiful waters, they were baptized, and an infant church was born—the first of many to follow.

———

In the next few years, the church multiplied. Alia had noticed that all the Kurdish women—most of whom were Muslim by tradition, although not by belief—were suffering from depression. While their husbands were able to get out of the house as often as they pleased, the wives were consigned to a prison-like existence, since Sharia law forbids women to appear in public except when accompanied by a male family member.

Respected as a brilliant scientist in her own right, Alia was able to move around the city as she pleased. Making appointments with different businessmen in town, she told them that she would like to build a center for women, including a workout room, where the Kurdish women could gather for fellowship and recreation. Through these and other contacts, she was able to raise $500,000, and the Ruth House was built and dedicated.

———

On our second trip to Kurdistan, Alia was overjoyed to show us around the new building. Inside the locker and workout rooms, she had installed pink carpet. We noticed that when the women took off their burqas, they decked themselves out in Hello Kitty loungewear, thinking this was the proper workout attire. These were doctors, computer programmers, teachers—women from different races and ethnicities. Alia had even located an Iranian woman to teach aerobics. At Ruth House, these women found community and loved each other despite any differences, and I fell in love all over again with the warm and friendly Kurdish people.

I learned that, outside their own country of Kurdistan, our city back home in Tennessee housed the largest population of Kurds in the world. Upon our return, we began reaching out to these refugees who had sought asylum in the land of the free. Our hearts were moved by their plight, and it wasn't long before some of us were sitting with Kurdish families on their living room rugs and sipping tea, ready to share with them the greatest news the world has ever known.

One Sunday, to my utter delight, an Assyrian woman—Layla, a former Bible student of Pastor Yousif's—walked into Belmont Church and back into my life. She was from Nineveh, Jonah's hometown. Seeing her again, I felt that our mission to Kurdistan had come full circle.

Romania—On-Site with Insight

I have long felt that while prayer is essential to any enterprise and must precede and cover a mission—on or off location—I prefer to have boots on the ground while interceding. I like to call it "on-site with insight." My first trip to Romania was no different.

In 1993, on my fiftieth birthday, I accompanied a group of sixty-two Belmont youth as one of their intercessors while in that Balkan country. The ministry team would be performing a production, "The Father's Dream," from their repertoire. It was an age-old tale of the first couple in their brand-new home, designed and decorated by God Himself. It was the perfect beginning. No other couple in all of human history would ever have it so good.

But you know the rest of the story. Satan, that low-down snake, did a home invasion and deceived the woman, and she got her first taste of sin. She handed off the evidence to her husband, and he took a bite. Now they were equally implicated and were soon evicted from their Garden apartment by their heavenly Land-Lord.

To reach their audiences, the kids would set up quickly in parks, train stations, and other public venues to tell the story of sin's entrance into the world. They would then finish with God's offer of redeeming love. Meanwhile, we intercessors prayed.

But it was not until we reached the mountainous region of Transylvania—this fascinating site of castles, fortresses, fortified churches, and mystical folklore—that we experienced the highlight of our trip. Under a hardcore communist dictator, Nicolae Ceausescu, many Christian pastors had been imprisoned. With the dictator's assassination a few years earlier, they had recently been released.

There was some kind of festival going on, and the pastors, filled with the fire of God, joined around five thousand young people in a celebration. Our presentation, a mime with music to carry the message, was new to this audience. The local pastor, in charge of the day-long event, was accustomed to a more traditional approach to the gospel and wanted to see a bit before signing off on it. As the kids swung into their version of the old-old story, I could see his countenance brighten. At the close of their audition, he clapped his hands and said, "Yes, let's do this!" Then and there we witnessed the church in this remote area embrace a move of God.

On a later trip, I prayed for a gypsy lady who didn't speak a word of English. I had no clue about this woman, yet the Holy Spirit translated, and she received the baptism of the Holy Spirit. I later learned that He came to her in the night and rained down on her. The next day, in a big church meeting, I spotted her across the room, wearing a brightly colored kerchief on her head. She broke out praying in tongues, glancing over at me. Her countenance was transformed with joy and delight.

In the following years, Belmont sent other teams into this area to harvest the fruit of our intercession. A bonus was our connection with a Christian TV station. During a conversation with a group of influential people, someone mentioned Don Finto's new book, *Your People Shall Be My People*, and left them a copy. The station secured a translator, and this on-time book was published in the Romanian language. What joy to sow, water, and then see the blossoming of the apostolic Christian ministry that was planted here.

Burma—High on Jesus

It was an unlikely group of folks—former drug dealers, users, and sellers, and a few intercessors. We were on our way to Burma, now called Myanmar, one of the three countries known as the

Golden Triangle in Southeast Asia. We were going there to pray over the region, which was famous for growing opium and was second only to Afghanistan in production. It was our hope that God would hear our prayers and cut off this source of some of the drugs that were flooding our country. More importantly, we would repent of America's role in drug trafficking.

At the border, we were asked to hand over our passports. I obliged without a second thought. Since there was no guarantee that the passports would be returned to us, one of the guys in our group asked me, "Are you going to give him your passport just like that?"

I shrugged. "That's what we have to do to get into their country to pray. Besides, I'd rather jump in the river and sink than be a bystander on the bank!"

Early the next morning—at 6:00 a.m. as agreed upon—we met in a park. At that hour, no one else was around that we could see, and we gathered in front of the huge statue of a soldier.

For the first few minutes, we worshipped, seeking direction for our prayers and acknowledging the One who could answer them. As the Spirit fell, the intensity of our worship and intercession increased and soon reached a fever pitch, with wailing and beating the ground.

Unnoticed by us, a couple of Asian gardeners, who had been pruning some shrubbery nearby, were alarmed by our behavior and approached to see if we needed them to call the police. They thought we were fighting among ourselves—or maybe high on drugs—but we assured them that we were friends, and no intervention was necessary.

While we did not see any overt signs of answered prayer during our time in Myanmar, when we returned home, it was no coincidence that the headlines in the Nashville newspaper the next day read: "Drug Raid on I-40!" It was the biggest drug bust in Tennessee history.

Prayer Journey to Northern Ireland

One intercessory venture took place in Northern Ireland at the invitation of John Alderdice of the House of Lords, United Kingdom. Lord Alderdice represented the part of Northern Ireland where President Andrew Jackson's ancestral home was located. Having been born again, Lord Alderdice was moved with compassion for the Native Americans who had been forcibly removed from their own land because of a bill signed by President Jackson. The infamous Trail of Tears was the heartbreaking result when these Native Americans were told that if they did not leave peacefully, they would be killed. It was Lord Alderdice's desire to acknowledge this tragedy and ask forgiveness of their descendants.

Since the treaty was signed in Franklin, Tennessee—my home for nearly fifty years—this was a very personal assignment for me. Therefore, I, along with forty others, including many Native Americans from the Yuchi, Cherokee, Choctaw, and the other Southern tribes, flew into Belfast to begin our week-long prayer vigil and to connect with like-minded citizens of this land. In addition, we were squired from city to city, where we met with the mayors and other dignitaries, along with local pastors, and treated to tea and dainties in customary Irish style.

At the Andrew Jackson estate, which was open to tourists, we experienced a chilling reminder of our reason for being here. The moment the First Nations people stepped onto the property, a wail went up like I have never heard. The sense of loss was almost tangible. How much the five Southern tribes had had to leave behind on the Trail of Tears—ostensibly making room for white settlers to establish their homes. That was only half the story; the newcomers planned to take over the land and make a profit.

Yet, despite all their losses, the Native Americans were the first to forgive. And here in Northern Ireland, thousands of miles from the scene of that dark stain on our history, Dr. Negiel Bigpond, apostolic pastor of Morning Star Church of All Nations in Oklahoma and leader of the Yuchi tribe, extended grace.

⸻

Eight years later, a resolution was drafted and signed by the Tennessee State Legislature, offering an apology to the Native Americans and inviting them to a reading of the resolution. The Lord spoke to some of us with specific instructions: *I want you to invite Lord Alderdice to this reading too.*

The Britisher accepted graciously. It would be his first visit to our state. The Native Americans had never been invited inside the Capitol building, and they responded eagerly to Kim Driver's invitation. From all over the country they came, dressed in full regalia—the chiefs in their feathered headdresses and fringed leather clothing, complete with beaded moccasins. Their drums echoed the thunder that was booming from the heavens.

The day of the reading brought a torrential downpour that lasted throughout the legislative session. Even with the First Nations people giving rapt attention to our request for forgiveness, they did not miss the special effects provided by the lightning flashing from overcast skies. It rained so hard that day that the water poured *inside* the building—a phenomenon that has not occurred since.

Some have explained this unusual weather event as "God's tears." But others have said, "He was washing off the bloodstains of that persecuted people group." Lord, forgive our sin against these brothers and sisters!

In 1975, during an address to a conference of First Nations leaders, Dr. Billy Graham had declared, "The greatest moments of Native History lie ahead of us if a great spiritual renewal and awakening should take place. The Native American has been a sleeping giant. The original Americans could become the evangelists who will help win America for Christ!"[5]

I would like to think that, in some way, we were contributing toward the fulfillment of that prophetic declaration.

Cuban Conquest

In the mid-1990s, Doug received a phone call from the South American head of the Jesus Film Project, the worldwide evangelistic outreach of Campus Crusade.

Having heard of our Bible-smuggling enterprise, he asked if we would be willing to accompany him in carrying some of the *Jesus* VHS tapes into Cuba. As it turned out, he was unable to secure a visa and it was up to the two of us and a few women from our church. No problem.

According to the repressive government at the time, it would be illegal for us to bring in Christian material from the United States. But this was nothing new. We had decided long ago that, in such cases, we would choose to heed the Word of God when Jesus said, "It is better to obey God rather than man." Therefore, another change of plans. We would cross the border into Mexico, join a tour group, and fly into Cuba from there. Once in Havana, we would simply slip away from the tour group and do our own thing.

Before we left, however, we had learned of the dire conditions in Cuba—especially among the persecuted Cuban Christians. Pastors' families had little to eat, and many of the wives could not attend church since they had no shoes—or even proper underwear. A quick trip to Marshall's, where we bought loads of shoes and other necessities, solved one problem. Then, at the grocery store, we stocked up on ham, rice, beans, and other food items, which we stuffed into duffel bags. In addition, Belmont Church collected $7,000 to bless needy Cubans as the Spirit led.

After arriving in Havana, Doug made a call from our room in the Riviera Hotel to the one contact we had been given. For some reason, this man insisted on meeting the two of us outside in his car.

Joining him as he had requested, we explained our mission—to get the *Jesus* film to as many Cubans as possible—then gave him some of the food we had brought. Before we left, Doug slipped him an envelope containing $1,000.

The man must have opened the envelope as soon as he arrived home, because our phone was ringing by the time we returned to our hotel room. "You come to *mi casa* tomorrow for lunch," he insisted. "And the money? Ha! That will be the bullet for my gun!"

We were not quite sure what he meant by that remark, but we were confident that he was a reliable contact. As always, we would simply trust the Lord. And the next day, when we showed up at this man's door, he invited us in with a big smile and a sweeping gesture. "Come in, come in," he said. "First we eat together, and then I show you how I operate."

Over lunch—dining on some of the food we had given him and feeling guilty for using up rations intended for hungry Cubans—we listened as he told us a little about himself. To our surprise, we learned that, as an eighteen-year-old, he had joined the Cuban Mafia. He still carried a powerful presence. No doubt that was why he had not been allowed to meet us in the hotel lobby.

After lunch, he invited us into his "headquarters." Hidden behind a wall was a secret recording studio where he made evangelistic tapes. So, the money sent by the church would be the "ammunition" for his ministry. This was no tough-guy Mafia member. This was an apostolic leader.

That night he showed the *Jesus* film to a large gathering of Cubans from his rooftop, probably the first outdoor theater in Cuba. We would leave many of the films in good hands.

In another place, Pines of the River, we found that a flood of Baptist pastors, some from America, were converging on the city for a conference. Since this was the rainy season and the host church needed a new roof, some of the money we had brought was given to re-roof the sanctuary and to purchase a video player to show the film.

In the process of becoming acquainted with this pastor and some of his congregation, I was invited to speak at the conference. In those days, no news from outside the country was allowed to reach the citizens. The situation for believers was grim. To register his disdain for Christianity, dictator Fidel Castro even had toilet paper made from the pages of Bibles.

It was my honor to bring these pastors up to speed. I shared with them some of my experiences among the persecuted Christians of China and other countries. It was eye-opening for many of them. For the first time, they realized that they were not the only ones suffering such persecution.

⸻

Holy Spirit was not through with us, though. Back in our hotel dining room, where a buffet dinner was being served, we found another opportunity to bless. While guests were invited to return to the buffet as often as we liked—each time with a different plate—we noticed something rather strange. To one side of the buffet table was a large dresser-like piece of furniture with several drawers, the top drawer remaining partly open.

After waitresses removed our plates, we spotted them scraping the leftovers into the drawer. Could this be how they were feeding their families?

Instantly, we knew what we must do. Each of us in our party returned to the buffet table to fill our plates, leaving the food untouched. When the waitresses asked if we were finished, we assured them that we were. Expressions of surprise changed to dawning understanding and then to joy and gratitude.

Sometimes the Spirit leads in obvious, in-your-face demonstrations of His power. But at other times, He shows us how to serve without saying a word.

Into All the World, But Begin at Home

If you are a child of the King, you know when you are being summoned. It may be a trumpet call to do great exploits in some faraway field. Or it may slip in when and where you least expect it—and be the very last thing you ever thought you would do.

One such call—quite literally—came on a Sunday when I was serving in the church nursery, which met in our pastor's study at the time. When I answered the phone, it was a lady named Pat who needed to speak with the pastor.

"I'm so sorry," I replied, "but he's preaching at the moment. Is there anything I can do to help you?"

There was—and we did.

When I offered to pick Pat up for church, she gave me the address of a home in a fashionable residential area in our city. Pulling up in front of the antebellum house, we discovered that our passenger-to-be lived in the caretaker's quarters at the back of the property. Leaving Doug and the boys in the car, I stepped onto the porch. Upon answering my knock, Pat stepped aside to let me in, and I could see a broken piggy bank on the table with a few coins scattered about. Not only was she destitute, but I learned that her living arrangements were only temporary; she was about to be evicted.

After church, on our way to take Pat back to her temporary residence, the summons that came to Doug was unmistakable, if slightly out of character for the King of the universe: *Put up or shut up,* He said. Obviously, Doug couldn't turn a deaf ear to this clear call to help the homeless, and we gathered her things and took her home with us.

There was more to her story, we learned that night around the dinner table. She was a drug addict. "Wanna see my track marks?" she asked our boys. Unaccustomed to the lingo, they thought she had been run over by a train.

Thus began a season none of us will ever forget. Two days later, Pat went into withdrawal. Hearing her moaning in the middle of the night, Doug took some Kenneth Copeland tapes and a tape player to the room where she was staying, with the instruction to call out if she needed further help.

Later the next morning, she emerged from the guest bedroom, wide-eyed and alert! "I'm healed!" she exclaimed. "I'm healed!"

She was, indeed, delivered from drugs overnight, it seemed, along with healing for a major back surgery we had heard nothing about until that moment!

The surprises were not over. Next thing we knew, Pat's brother called, saying he had had a fire in his apartment and needed a place to stay "temporarily." Doug and I suspected that Pat had alerted him to the fact that she had found a port in the storm. Brother Kenneth was followed by Pat's husband…and their dog!

Two or three days after that, a sheriff's deputy showed up at our door with a warrant for Pat's arrest. When I discreetly explained what was going on and that we were trying to help her, he tucked the warrant back in his pocket and said, "You not only saved a life, you saved a soul." He left without ever telling us what the warrant was for.

From June until October of that year, we had four lodgers, and I was chief cook—three square meals a day, plus doggy food!

In the fall, though, it was time for our tenants to move on. Doug, kind-hearted man that he is, didn't let her go empty-handed, but gave her a car. We didn't see Pat again until several months later when she called to tell us that she was living in a trailer park on

Dickerson Pike. She was experiencing a rough patch and needed a safe place to stay for a while. She came. She stayed. For a while. By herself this time.

—

There is something about me and laundry because the Lord has chosen—more than once—to speak to me when I am busy with this chore. This time, when I passed Pat in the hall on my way to the laundry room, lugging a basket of dirty clothes, I caught a whiff of the most marvelous perfume. "Great fragrance," I told her. "You smell just like roses."

She shook her head. "Not wearing any perfume."

That afternoon, she told me about an amazing visitor she had met. "*Jesus* was in my room!" she said. "First, He stood at the foot of my bed and smiled at me. Then He moved to the side of the bed, sat down, and hugged me for the longest time." Choking on tears, she could barely utter the words. "I've been rejected all my life, and He told me that He took my rejection on the cross and I would never know rejection again."

Ah, so it was the fragrance of the Lord I had smelled.

He did not stop with that blessing for Pat. Not long afterward, someone gave her a brick house. A prostitute friend from the past offered Pat her newborn baby she could not afford to keep, and a dentist fixed her teeth, black from years of drug use—at no charge. What a dramatic turnaround for a homeless woman. All that—yet nothing compared to being born again and filled with the Spirit of Jesus who had hugged her in my guest room.

Several years earlier, in a small group, a prophet named Mahesh Chavda had prophesied that Doug and I would "take the gospel to the nations . . . and experience a visitation of the Lord in our home." Mahesh was right on both counts.

Chapter 9

That None
Should Perish

The Lord is . . . longsuffering toward us,
not willing that any should perish
but that all should come to repentance.

2 Peter 3:9

I love to connect the dots—you know, that childhood game where a picture is formed by tracing a line from one number to the next. It was always so exciting to discover the picture that would emerge at the end of the activity. (No way would I have ever been able to draw a horse otherwise!)

I especially love to follow Holy Spirit's dots, never knowing where He will lead—or when. One year, He sent two of us—Sisse Pfieffer and me—to Mozambique, at one time the poorest and most war-torn country in the world. It was here, to this area on the southeastern coast of Africa, that Drs. Rolland and Heidi Baker had been called to minister to abandoned street children. And it is this husband-and-wife team who founded Iris Global, a ministry that has subsequently expanded to reach the destitute and forgotten in countries around the world.

Not being responsible for leading a group on this trip, Sisse and I found ourselves happily playing armor-bearer to two women who had been invited to teach at a conference in the Bakers' Harvest School—Jill Austin of the Kansas City Prophets and Michal Ann Goll, author, speaker, and the late wife of James Goll. Jill had once prophesied that I should be ordained, but I saw no purpose in that as I have always been content to simply "follow the dots" at the Spirit's prompting. In fact, our purpose in making this journey was to intercede for the students in this school and, as we learned, to assist the two speakers in their evangelistic mission to take the Word to the people in outlying villages. (Only much later did I follow up on Jill's suggestion that I be ordained.)

At least sixty students had gathered for this conference in the second of what would be thirty-five such training schools over the next decades. But it was still early in the school's development, and we met in a primitive tent with only the reddish-brown sand for a floor.

As Prophetess Jill Austin prophesied over a young Asian man, he fell back and began spinning in circles while lying on the ground. Jill described what we were seeing: "An angel is playing with him, twirling and spinning him. He has no control over what is happening."

At that, hilarious laughter erupted from the audience. It was obvious that it would have been impossible to spin and twirl on that sandy dirt floor without angelic assistance, and in those moments, everyone in the class witnessed the supernatural power of God.

That was only the beginning of the signs and wonders the Spirit would unfold. After the teaching that morning, followed by the demonstration of His power, Rolland Baker prayed for the students. His petition was so fervent, it was as if he were on a heavenly pogo stick. Each time Rolland prayed, he jumped so high it seemed that a holy Tigger had hold of him.

Every evening for the next two weeks, we climbed into the backs of pickup trucks to drive into the bush and the bush-bush (deep bush)—with generators and a movie projector—to show the *Jesus* film to the indigenous people. There was not a night without multiple conversions of these precious souls. Worth every mile of the trips through dense forest. A bonus was getting to know Heidi and Rolland Baker and to appreciate their ministry and sacrificial lives of worship and humility.

———

On second thought, maybe God is more of a chess player than a "follow-the-dot" Creator. In His brilliance, He is always many moves ahead of us. Yet, in His wisdom, He does not tell us everything He is doing at the time. Years later, in 2016, I was asked to bring one hundred of Heidi's books to a conference in Thailand, where she would address some of the very people she had trained in her ministry schools. The conference-goers came from all over Asia—China, Burma, Korea, the Philippines—so many of those who had said yes to God because of Heidi and Rolland Baker.

Russia! Russia! Russia!

For some time—from the Cold War years to the more recent crisis in Ukraine—the prospect of Russia triggering a nuclear holocaust has been a clear and present danger. But in September 2001, it was not Russia that staged an attack on our soil. It was radical terrorists from another country.

That month, hundreds of intercessors from all over the world were scheduled to travel to a conference in Hanover, Germany, after which all of us would be dispersed to the nations to pray for a release of global fire. With the tragic events of 9/11, though, most of those who had planned to represent our church dropped out. Only eleven of us, including Mike Pfieffer, Carol Goodwin, Doug, and I, made the trip.

We had been invited by Peter Wagner, and the plan was to gather first in Germany to meet with Peter, Cindy Jacobs, James

Goll, and other leaders to prepare for the prayer journey. From there, our team would fly to Moscow.

Before the conference in Germany got underway, in what could only have been a divine appointment, Doug chatted with Fatima Robinson, a native of the Middle East. She and her husband, David, had been sent out from our church as missionaries to Pakistan, the nation bordering India and Afghanistan. For the past twenty-five years, the Robinsons had lived and worked among the Pakistani people under the auspices of the NGO Shelter Now International. Due to heightened tensions in the region, they had left their post temporarily, and Fatima was attending this conference.

What happened next was definitely one of those "dots" God had planted ahead of time. I'll let Doug tell that story.

Doug: I'll never forget the day I saw Fatima entering the meeting room and making her way toward me. At that moment, Dabney was chatting with someone in another part of the room and would catch up later. As I sensed the Spirit's presence, my eyes filled with tears.

In my conversation with Fatima, we discussed the recent kidnapping of two young American women—Dayna Curry and Heather Mercer—by the Taliban. The two girls were Christian aid workers, also working under the German missionary group Shelter Now. Moved by the plight of women in Afghanistan, they had volunteered to go there to help the poor, especially widows and orphans.

In the process, they had also shown the Jesus *film to unbelievers, who were hungry to know about the One who could rescue them from the wrath of God and give them a new life. Consequently, the two girls had been accused of preaching the gospel of Christ in this strictly Islamist state and had been held in Taliban prisons under harsh conditions for the past three months. The situation was dire.*

"Have you heard anything about those two U.S. aid workers by any chance?" I asked.

To my surprise, the answer was, "Yes! In fact, a young Afghan man smuggled a satellite phone into the compound where the girls are being held, and he has been secretly updating us on their situation. I have that number."

There was no time for more, as the seminar had started. But Holy Spirit was not through. The last speaker was a major in the U.S. military, a chaplain with Delta Force, trained in special ops. As soon as the meeting was adjourned and the major stepped down from the platform, I met him at the front.

Wasting no time with introductions, I said, "Follow me. I have something for you—the phone number where the two aid workers are being contained."

His reply was priceless. "My people at Fort Bragg will know about that before the sun goes down."

On the way to the place where Fatima was seated, I decided that I would introduce the two of them and let her handle the transfer of information. Introductions made, I quickly bowed out. This was holy ground—too holy for me to touch.

Using Fatima's information, the two girls were rescued just weeks later by the U.S. military. Only God could have connected these dots.

———

Upon arriving in Moscow, we prayed with other on-fire intercessors, toured historic sites, and prayed some more. At the Moscow State Historical and Cultural Museum, where the wealth of former dynasties was on full display, the disparity between the haves and the have-nots could not have been more striking. Here we saw the thrones of former kings and queens, ermine-trimmed robes, diamond-encrusted crowns, and even coaches with 24-karat gold-studded wagon wheels. I couldn't help thinking, *Someone ought to have a garage sale!* It was mind-boggling to consider that the government would keep all that loot locked away while so many of their citizens starved to death through the centuries.

Still, our hearts went out to the wounded Russian soldiers, veterans of the protracted war with Afghanistan. The deeper wound—one that needed to be reopened and cleansed so it could heal—was the part the United States played in that war. During a visit with a Messianic Jewish congregation in the city, Cindy Jacobs confessed that our country had invaded Afghanistan. She then called us up to ask for their forgiveness, which blessed the Russians tremendously. In retrospect, that might have been the most important accomplishment of the entire trip.

Bound for Bangladesh

On an early morning in 2012, the phone rang. When I answered, a familiar voice came from the other end of the line. The message was both thrilling and troubling. "Dabney," he began, "would you be willing to come to Dhaka, Bangladesh, to teach the women of a house church there?"

By now, you know that I would go anywhere, anytime to reach people for Jesus, but right off the bat, I could think of several good reasons why this time might not be one of them.

"Oh, you don't need *me*. I can tell you the right person for this assignment. Her name is Fatima Robinson. The Robinsons have lived in Eastern Asia for twenty-five years and she knows the language and—"

But my friend was adamant. "No, *you're* the right person, Dabney. These women have been taught to hate—Jews, Christians, anyone who does not share their Islamic beliefs. And many of them need deliverance—something you and Doug have taught for years in your church."

When we hung up from this conversation, I had tentatively agreed to go, still feeling some reservations. A quick Google search gave further pause. This was the land of ferocious Bengal tigers who could crush every bone in the human body with one snap of their massive jaws. In addition, there were bandits who threatened unsuspecting travelers and monsoons that flooded the streets of the cities so that moving about was virtually impossible. But it wasn't like me to consider the dangers.

As it turned out, knowing the opportunity to reach this disenfranchised population, Doug and I made the trip together.

———

Contrary to expectations, my first encounter with the women of Bangladesh was delightful. Rather than the dreary, black burqas and head coverings worn by many women with their Muslim background, these believers from the house church were wearing robes and head scarves in beautiful, bright colors. As their faces were not covered, I could see their lovely golden skin and flashing smiles, noting the whiteness of their teeth.

When I told them my age—seventy at the time—they could not believe that I still had all *my* teeth, which was rare in their culture.

Off to this glorious start, I felt led to begin with a "show and tell" to help them understand that Israel is no threat to them, rather the apple of God's eye with a global purpose. Prior to this journey, I had made a trip to Walmart to purchase a world map on fabric that could be folded up and packed in my suitcase. Using this prop, I pointed out the size of tiny Israel as compared to the much larger nation of Bangladesh.

"Why hate this very small country?" I asked. "Now, let me tell you why we should not hate them, rather be grateful to God for them."

With that, I launched into a parable the Lord had given me. "Suppose a father had many children, some of whom didn't listen to him. Instead, they did their own thing, went their own way. Finally, in desperation, this father decided, 'What if I take the eyes from my own children and give them to some orphans in the street so the orphans can see my love and good deeds and turn to me and obey me?'

119

"The orphans were now able to see him while his natural-born children became jealous. You are the 'orphans,' and God has revealed Himself to you so that many in Israel will be jealous and want what you've been given—an understanding of the ways of God. Yet, Israel has preserved the written Word for millennia and is the birthplace of the Savior. So, you see, those who know Him and love Him, as you do, owe a debt of gratitude to Israel."

These women loved Jesus; until now, they just hadn't understood seeing with the eyes of the heart. They got it. They loved what they heard, and I was able to lead them in true repentance for their unforgiving spirit toward God's Chosen People.

Following this victory, Doug and I taught on deliverance from evil spirits. Using role play, we told the women how Jesus, through the Holy Spirit, had given believers the power to cast out tormenting spirits. Then we demonstrated how to use the Word to expel the demonic. One of us would speak the liberating Word while the other "coughed out" the demon.

When the demonstration ended, some of the men, who had waited around to see what was going to happen, applauded. The Spirit was truly in that place, giving us favor.

That January, even before the invitation to Bangladesh, I had asked God to allow me to do two things for Him: (1) to teach illiterate women about God since they could not read about Him for themselves, and (2) to be part of drilling a well somewhere in the world so the people could have clean water.

The first request was granted on that trip. Part two came after we returned home. We had learned that when the United Nations decided on the border between Bangladesh and Pakistan, they had dug some wells, but had never tested the water for heavy metals. As a result, half the population of Bangladesh suffered from arsenic poisoning, along with arthritis and even cancer.

With this information, we were able to raise enough funds to dig *two* wells, making sure the water was filtered for harmful elements. I am so glad I didn't turn down this trip.

Israel—Land of Promise

Over the past forty years, it has been my privilege to travel to Israel many times, the first in 1979, led by Derek Prince, who was present when Israel was declared a nation by President Truman. Dr. Prince, the renowned Bible scholar and author, taught us that God loved Israel. In those early days of faith, that was good enough for me—so I loved Israel too. Since then, we have grown in our understanding of God's plan and purpose for Israel as a light to the Gentiles. Therefore, each trip is both a renewal and a revelation.

In 1983, Doug and I were in Jerusalem. On our last evening in the city, there was to be some kind of celebration at midnight at the Western Wall, the most sacred site in all of Judaism. This is where people from around the world come to pray, often depositing written prayers on slips of paper in the cracks and crevices of the ancient wall.

Since we were to board our flight for the return trip early the next morning, we decided not to go to bed, but packed our suitcases and hired a taxi driver for the evening to take us to the Wall. We planned to arrive by 11:00 p.m. so as not to miss anything.

When we reached the Wall, whatever was about to unfold was still a mystery to us, as there were few people around. But promptly at the stroke of midnight, we heard what sounded like the rumble of an approaching train. A quick glance over our shoulders revealed a train of *people*—singing at the top of their voices. Some of the men were hoisting rabbis, replete in tallits (prayer shawls) and yarmulkes (small round head coverings), on their shoulders. Pulling up at about the same time were black limousines, Israeli flags flying, bringing other officials to the gathering.

We learned that this festive occasion was being held to commemorate the twenty-fifth anniversary of the 1967 Six-Day War—a brief conflict between Israel and some of her Arab neighbors (Egypt, Syria, and Jordan), in which much of God's original blueprint for His Chosen People's homeland was reclaimed. Thousands now thronged the area to celebrate what He had done a quarter of a century earlier. Since that evening, we have come to understand that this is an annual event called Reunification Day.

On another trip with Pastor Steve Fry, during the Feast of Tabernacles, we traveled to the marvelous outdoor amphitheater at Beit-She'an. Here, an Israeli troupe presented an original Broadway-style musical, *Thy Kingdom Come,* written by Steve, who also performed in the production. The musical featured many actors, along with live camels and donkeys. Thousands came for the performance.

This was also the first time that a large number of Christians had ever traveled to Jerusalem to pray in the Knesset rose garden at the invitation of leading rabbis. Later in the day, walking up the stone steps to intercede with the crowd of 3,500 others, I heard the Lord say to me, *You will not see Me again until you hear Me say, "Blessed is he who comes in the name of the Lord."*

It was a glorious time of praise and worship with such dignitaries as Pat Robertson, Jack Hayford, and Robert Stearns, the founder of Eagles Wings Ministries and the man who established the National Day of Prayer for Jerusalem. Photographers were milling about to snap pictures of the event, including someone from the magazine *Vanity Fair.* This photographer caught me in an unrehearsed posture of praise at one point. While I would never have posed for such a picture, of course, the photo is a lasting reminder of an experience that is now forever etched in my memory.

i

For several years, Don Finto's organization, Caleb Global, maintained a condominium in Jerusalem for the benefit of those making ministry trips to Israel. On at least three occasions, when I led groups of women to the Holy Land, we were invited to stay there. This condo was our home away from home while attending the Feast of Tabernacles in Jerusalem another year.

Seeing the prejudice toward women still evident in the very land where Jesus had elevated them by being born of a woman, was disturbing. The inequality was glaringly obvious at the Western Wall. The men's and women's prayer sections are sharply divided because of the gender segregation promoted by ultra-Orthodox Jews. When passing by earlier, we had noticed that the men's side was crowded, and they were loud and raucous. Some of them were wearing their tasseled prayer shawls and dancing with the Torah held aloft. On the women's side, the number was much smaller and more subdued. No singing and dancing.

Back home in our church in Nashville, I had been asked to head a women's group the elders had tentatively titled "Caleb's Daughters." I agreed to pray about it. In the Bible, Caleb's daughter's name was Achsah. When I looked up the meaning in a concordance, I found that Achsah means "adornment such as an ankle bracelet." The definition sounded okay, if a bit trivial. But another definition was "bursting the veil." That was more like it. We could work with that. And an idea was born: We would purchase a veil and rip it to shreds, giving each woman a piece to "sow into" the Wall along with our prayers for the peace of Jerusalem—and freedom for all.

The last day of the Feast, on our way to the Wall, we stopped in a little bridal shop to purchase a veil. The first price mentioned was a staggering $500 in American money.

"Don't you have something much less expensive?" I asked,

knowing we only intended to rip it up anyway. "Maybe one that is damaged?"

We left with our $15 purchase and headed to the Wall to tear the veil into small pieces.

In the Plaza area, at the entrance to the Wall, we formed a circle, giving each woman a piece of the veil. With security tight in this sacred season, we were careful not to draw attention to ourselves, but walked down to the Wall slowly and discreetly.

In this holy place, with access to the power and Presence of God like no other, we walked over to pray and to deposit our prayers in the form of the torn veil, asking God to watch over His people and to tear the veil from their eyes regarding His Son. But just to make sure He also considered the plight of His daughters, I stuck my piece of veil in the niche directly between the men's and women's sections of the prayer wall, asking Him to give favor to the women—Jews, Muslims, and Christians alike.

As for the veil, a great deal of it was left over, and I threw it in my suitcase and took it home with me. Several years later, Rachel McDowell, wife of Tod McDowell, president of Caleb Global, became the leader of Caleb's Daughters. I felt led to give the remainder of the veil to her—as a torch handed off to the next generation of leaders.

When It Is Time to Go . . .

Before we left the Wall that night, we located a cab for hire with an Arab driver. Abdul spoke broken English. Fortunately for us, Fatima Robinson was with our group and could converse freely with him in Farsi.

She gave him the address of the condominium where we had been staying, and he immediately broke into a wide grin. "I know that place. You won't believe this, but *believe* it. It is true. My brother and I were with the security team while that condo was being built."

Coincidence? I doubt it. Once again, the Lord had prepared the way before us, even providing a trained security guard in this holiest of seasons when Arabs and Jews often clash as they celebrate the festivals of their respective faiths.

Before we paid Abdul and said goodnight, Fatima added, "Sir, there is a place we would like to visit tomorrow—Hebron."

"No problem," he said. "I return for you in the morning. *Shab bekheir, sayidat!*" With a courtly bow and a flourish of his hand, he was off.

True to his word, Abdul arrived at our doorstep promptly at 8:00 the next morning for the short trip to Hebron. This biblical city is located in Palestinian territory in the occupied West Bank, some twenty miles south of Jerusalem. But the trip took longer than anticipated since the roads in that region are primitive and there were so many security stops.

With the escalating tensions in those days and the threat of terrorism, there were no other tourists, and we had the run of the place. The possibility of danger has rarely bothered me, but in addition to our self-appointed security guard, we felt the presence of angelic escort.

It was utterly delightful to stroll through the Jewish synagogue, side by side with an Islamic mosque, and to visit the burial site of Abraham and his beloved Sarah, along with the resting places of other patriarchs. We took our time, praying in the Spirit, dedicating every inch of this soil back to the One who had created it and marked out its boundaries as His own.

When we returned to Jerusalem at the end of the day, we had one more request. "Abdul, could you take us to the Pool of Siloam tomorrow?"

"Of course," he replied with enthusiasm. "It is only about five minutes from here. I take you!"

Still reveling in all we had seen and heard that day and with the sweet connection we were making with our new Arab friend, our sleep was fitful at best. We rose early, eager to see the Pool of Siloam in the Old City of David.

Abdul was right. This historic pool—its freshwater spring originating from somewhere beneath the Temple Mount, it is said—was only a short distance from our condo. It was thrilling to be in the actual spot where the man born blind washed his eyes after Jesus anointed them with mud. Once Jesus healed the man, he could see. Our silent prayer was that Yeshua would remove the scales from the eyes of our new friend Abdul as well.

When an elderly Arab gentleman suddenly appeared from a nearby gift shop, Abdul introduced him as "Uncle." On the way over from the hotel, Abdul had told us that the land surrounding the Pool had belonged to his family for six generations. No doubt they were well respected in the community. What an incredible journey we were on! Holy Spirit's "dots" continued to amaze us.

Knowing that we would be leaving the country soon, we were dreading the moment when we would have to leave this place. There would be other trips to Israel in the future, but perhaps none more precious than this one where we had sown our prayers—and our tears.

Chapter 10

Saved, Sealed, and Set Free!

"These signs will follow those who believe:
In My name they will cast out demons;
They will speak with new tongues; . . .
They will lay hands on the sick, and they will recover."
Mark 16:17–18

Early on, it was never Doug's and my intention to launch a formal deliverance ministry, characterized by "casting out demons." That would mean confronting the spiritual powers of darkness head-on. A scary thought—and one for which I was eminently unqualified. Well, except for the fact that both Doug and I understood firsthand that demonic attacks can happen to anyone—even Spirit-filled believers. It happened to us.

Shortly after moving to Nashville, Tennessee, we attended a weekend seminar conducted by Derek Prince at a local Holiday Inn. His message was so powerful that both Doug and I were delivered from some form of bondage, then baptized in water in the outdoor hotel swimming pool. In February, no less! Luckily for us, one of the warmest on record. We hadn't come prepared with a change of clothes, so we were dunked as is—Doug in his suit and tie, and I in my dress and pantyhose.

As for me, I hadn't felt I needed deliverance. But hearing Dr. Prince's message that night—how evil spirits can even attack born-again believers in some vulnerable spot—I knew I *did* need it. I had picked up a spirit of rejection in childhood, which made it difficult to receive or to give love. Much to my joy and relief, I was supernaturally freed from this spirit that had a stranglehold on my life.

Shortly after our conversion and later on, between mission trips, Doug and I hosted a group of fired-up new Christians in our home, as you learned earlier in this book. May I remind you that this group was not a formal "small group" sanctioned by our church necessarily. It had simply spilled over from a weekend seminar.

We were all soaking in the Word, hungry to learn everything we could about this Jesus who loved us enough to die for us. Now we wanted to serve and follow Him in obedience—sharing the gospel and bringing healing and deliverance to others. We just didn't know how.

"Even Greater Things"

To acquire anything new about the ways of the Lord, a believer only has to be desperate. And we were desperate. He met us at the point of our need and had sent this amazing man of God to our city.

Derek Prince's subject for the seminar—casting out demons—was based on Scripture. Jesus' last recorded words in the Gospel of Mark are, *"And these signs will accompany those who believe: In My name they will drive out demons"* (Mark 16:17). Let me be clear, though: Before we undertake to minister a deliverance, we must have a personal, intimate relationship with the Father, empowered by the Holy Spirit. It's His love that compels us to rid ourselves and others of anything that is not of Him.

Dr. Prince prefaced his remarks by pointing out all the

instances in which Jesus Himself had delivered people from demonic oppression or possession. At least one hundred times in the New Testament, words referring to evil spirits/demons are mentioned. Then, without question, Jesus authorized believers to go and do likewise: "I have given you authority . . . to overcome all the power of the enemy" (Luke 10:19 niv). In fact, He went a step further: "Very truly I tell you, whoever believes in me will do the works I have been doing, and they will do *even greater things* than these, because I am going to the Father" (John 14:12 niv).

As you may recall, during those early sessions led by Derek Prince, Doug had taken notes, and it was these notes, plus material gleaned from other authors and teachers on the subject, that formed the basis for the deliverance seminar the two of us were asked to lead in our church several years later.[6]

We absorbed everything we could possibly find on the subject. When we discovered that Dr. Prince also had a lending library of his cassette teaching tapes, we ordered them and listened together several times a week at our group meeting. One of our number even flew to Fort Lauderdale, Florida, where he was living at the time, and bought $75 worth of his cassette tapes to bring back to share. We just couldn't get enough.

Meanwhile, word had gotten out about our weekly sessions. People were showing up at our house to ask for prayer, and many were healed or set free from some demonic entity. One of the first was a woman who had lost a loved one and felt she was being harassed by a spirit of grief.

Midway through the deliverance, we discerned that it was her own personal grief she was carrying. At that point, we changed direction and addressed her need to process her pain. This process is unique for each individual, but in her case, we found that she was harboring resentment against God. "He could have healed my husband," she cried. She had to forgive Him and allow Him to heal her—or open herself to full demonic attack. An evil spirit will pounce on an unhealed wound like a fly on an infection, so it is important to discover the root of a person's problem.

Some of these sessions with those who were truly "demonized"—not demon-possessed—were rather dramatic, with screams, groans, or tears as demons were bound, made their exit, and sent to the "dry places." Our boys were quite young at the time, and they later confessed to being terrified. As a result, I would not recommend that couples conduct deliverances within the hearing distance of small children.

On the other hand, as young as they were, my boys picked up on the desperate needs of these people and even some of the deliverance language Doug and I used. (More about that in the following section.) I will never forget the afternoon when a lady dropped by unexpectedly while Doug was away at work. Little Drew—then three years old—climbed up on the couch and scooted over beside me, declaring, "Mom, you get the woot (root), and I'll get the spiwit!"

Learning the Lingo

From our personal experience and the testimony of others, we quickly found that one question surfaced on a fairly regular basis: "Is it possible for a Christian to be indwelt by an evil spirit/demon?" We had asked it ourselves. The answer is found in the following verses. When Jesus was addressing Peter once, He said, "Get behind Me, Satan!" (Matthew 16:23). And there were Ananias and Sapphira, who were asked, "Why has Satan filled your heart?" (Acts 5:3). These were either disciples who loved Jesus or followers who revered Him, yet they were sideswiped by Satan or one of his minions.

But what, exactly, are these evil entities?

- Demon, in ancient, pagan Greece, was used to describe a disembodied spirit—actually, according to

Dr. Prince, a person with a personality—seeking a body through whom to live, deceive, and eventually destroy. Demons are not ideas, thought patterns, or theories. They are actual beings. Jesus dealt with them as one would speak to some lower form of animal life.

- Evil, or unclean, spirit is a breath-like being that comes to defile, torment, and harass. These evil spirits are intended to conform a person to their image rather than allowing the Holy Spirit to conform the person to the image of Jesus Christ. For the purposes of our deliverance ministry, we use these first three demonic titles interchangeably.
- Strongholds are systems of thought, false beliefs, brought about by demonic influences.
- Curses are the opposite of blessings and are usually passed down through the generations. Sometimes, simply speaking negative words can produce a curse, as words have the power to bring life or death.
- Yokes, snares, and bondages are invisible barriers that prevent us from living a fruitful life in the Spirit.

Evil spirits have names. Remember the man from Gadara who was tormented by demons so cruelly that he lived among the tombs in that region? Even chains could not contain him. (For the full story, see Mark 5:1–20.)

When Jesus approached him, He spoke to the demon (not to the man), "'Come out of the man, unclean spirit!' Then He asked him, 'What is your name?' And he answered Him, 'My name is Legion, for we are many'" (vv. 8–9).

I will not list all the names of demonic spirits here. But take my word for it: there are almost too many to mention. They sometimes come in clusters or families, with all their tagalong relatives. Take the spirit of depression, for example. This one may come with the spirits of loneliness, disappointment, misery, and even suicide. While there may be some medical component too, one or more of these spirits may be hijacking the diagnosis. Never rule out the possibility of demonic involvement since the enemy, in his many disguises, is always on the prowl "seeking whom he may devour" (1 Peter 5:8).

———

Derek Prince once told of a young woman who needed deliverance when he was ministering in Seattle, Washington. When she was brought to him on a Saturday morning (along with her Baptist pastor and some friends, a Presbyterian couple), she appeared to be quite calm, intelligent, and rational. In fact, she was a member of the church staff.

Since this was one of his first experiences with deliverance—and in front of an unlikely audience in that time—Dr. Prince cried out to the Holy Spirit for help. Following the example of Jesus, he addressed the spirit, not the woman, using the authority Jesus has granted all believers: "In the name of Jesus, I command you to come out, you foul spirit."

No response. The woman (or the spirit) remained completely silent.

Dr. Prince repeated the command. "In Jesus' name, come out of her!" Then he remembered to ask for the spirit's name. "What is your name, you unclean spirit?"

To everyone's surprise, this lovely woman's face suddenly contorted, and out of her mouth came a gruff, masculine-sounding growl: "My name is Hate, and I'm not coming out! This is my house! I have lived here for thirty-five years!"

When he used the spirit's name, he left her with a loud roar, shouting, "I will come out, but my brothers are still here!"

It was two or three hours later before the woman was finally set free, and it was a struggle.

This is not necessarily the typical scenario. Most deliverances are much milder, but we need to be aware that we are dealing with real, though invisible persons who are strong, stubborn, and determined to stay right where they are.

——

May I give you another illustration of deliverance—this time, deliverance from a generational curse? One day we received a phone call from a woman named Marie who was harassed by a spirit of suicide, and arranged to meet with her on a Saturday afternoon.

"In my family, people kill themselves," she informed us when she arrived at our door.

After hearing her story, Doug suddenly exclaimed, "In the name of Jesus, I break the curse of suicide over you!"

In my mind, I saw some kind of satellite swirling in the atmosphere above this woman. The satellite was sending this message over and over, "Kill yourself! Kill yourself!"

A few minutes later, after speaking the Word of God over her and using Jesus' name, we disarmed the curse, and she went on her way rejoicing.

Within six months, she called again and asked if we would stop by her house so that she could share what God had done since our time together. We were eager to hear.

"This past summer, I attended our family reunion in North Carolina," she began. "You need to know that I have—or *had*—three brothers. The two remaining ones, who live at opposite ends of the state of California, were at the reunion. The twin of one of them committed suicide some time ago. My older brother—a medical doctor in Southern California—was freed from the spirit of suicide while working in his garden. My other brother, from Northern California, was freed from that same spirit and, at the same time, relieved of the haunting question as to why his twin had killed himself."

"When was this?" we wanted to know.

"The morning of the day you prayed for my deliverance."

Knowing that the time zone in California—Pacific Standard—is a few hours earlier than Eastern time, we were stunned. It was the exact same time of our prayer for their sister. And we were not even in the same state, nor were the two brothers in the same location. When we released God's Word into the atmosphere, the Sword of the Spirit sailed across the country, through three time zones, and cut that evil thing to shreds!

"We do not wrestle against flesh and blood, but against principalities, against powers, against the rulers of the darkness of this age. Against spiritual hosts of wickedness in the heavenly places" (Ephesians 6:12).

How Demons Get in the Door

I had been saved only two or three months and was a mom with a four-year-old and a newborn when the Lord taught me a lesson on how demons get into a person. I have never forgotten it. In one of our many moves in those days, we had recently moved into a new home, and I had not yet had time to meet anyone in the neighborhood. So I had no way of knowing the territory—which families might have pets, whether there were leash laws in this area, et cetera.

One morning, with Doug away at work, I needed to make a run to the grocery store. After bundling up the two little boys, I made my way to the car through the front door, buckled the toddler into his car seat and the baby in his infant seat, then realized that I had left my purse in the house. As I stepped back inside, I was greeted by a huge black lab that lunged toward me, nearly knocking me off my feet.

There were muddy pawprints everywhere, and I had no time to clean up the mess. I don't know where he had come from, and I never saw him again. All I wanted was to get him out of my house! Apparently, I had left the door open in my haste to get the children in the car.

This "parable" came to mind when Doug and I were dealing with the demonic in people who were asking for deliverance. When you encounter an intruder—in the natural or supernatural—you just want them out.

We would soon learn just how many "doors" we may inadvertently leave open, giving access to the enemy of our souls. We will mention several, capitalizing many of them to remind us that they are actual persons looking for bodies to inhabit.

- **The Occult, Sorcery, and Witchcraft**—God calls this arena of satanic power "spiritual adultery" since we are seeking knowledge and powers apart from Him (see Exodus 21:3–5). Common entry points for demonic spirits are consulting fortunetellers or psychics, séances, Ouija boards, horoscopes, astrology, palm reading, tea leaves, and tarot cards. Sorcery can include Substance Abuse (drugs and/or alcohol), Charms, Magic, and some forms of sensual or secular music. Then there is blatant Witchcraft, including Satan Worship, which is gaining momentum in our day. The rise of Abortion, Sex Trafficking, and Gender Confusion, often aided and funded by those in high offices in our land, indicates how far America has fallen. A Jezebel spirit would also come under the category of Witchcraft. This spirit seeks to usurp God-appointed authority and seat itself in that place. It is known to emasculate men, and some believe this spirit to be at the root of Homosexuality.
- **Rebellion**—This spirit is a close cousin of Witchcraft. In fact, Rebellion may even be its twin. The Bible couldn't be clearer: "Rebellion is as the sin of

witchcraft" (1 Samuel 15:23). This spirit and the host of others that follow it are usually there because of Pride. An attitude that says, "Nobody is going to tell me what to do!" will open us up for this one. Some spirits associated with Pride and Rebellion are Anger, Hatred, Rage, Violence, Murder, Independence, Arrogance, Control, and Fear.

- **Generational Sins**—We are warned in Scripture, "I, the LORD your God, am a jealous God, punishing the children for the sins of the fathers to the third and fourth generation of those who hate [Me], but showing love to a thousand generations of those who love [Me] and keep [My] commandments" (Exodus 20:5–6 NIV). Certain genetic weaknesses that contribute to some illnesses are actually demonic spirits and need to be cast out before a person can be healed. There are many other generational sins, including Alcoholism and Drug Abuse, which are also named under Sorcery.
- **Trauma**—Some sins are committed against us by others. These would include Child Abuse, Pedophilia, Rape, Divorce, and Family Dysfunction of all kinds. "For where envying and strife is, there is confusion and every evil work" (James 3:16 KJV). Just remember, these spirits thrive on unhealed wounds. In such cases, spiritual "surgery"—confessing, cleansing, and treating—may be required before the demon can be cast out. This is known as inner healing.[7] It is important to note that inner healing and deliverance go hand in hand. The person praying needs to be discerning as to the source of the problem.
- **Rejection**—A person demonized by this spirit will generally have trouble believing that God or anyone

else could really love them, and this opens the way for many other spirits, such as Loneliness, Depression, Self-pity, Condemnation, Insecurity, Inferiority, and even Suicide. Sadly, this spirit will also make it nearly impossible for a person *to give* genuine love to others.

- **Sins of the Flesh**—While some of these may be actual evil spirits or demons, again we have to be discerning as to whether our own weak flesh is at fault or an evil spirit has actually entered. Sometimes, it is both—a weakness of the flesh is an open invitation for the spirit to come on in. The list seems endless and is sobering, but we quote directly from God's Word: "Now the works of the flesh are evident, which are adultery, fornication, uncleanness, lewdness, idolatry, sorcery, hatred, contentions, jealousies, outbursts of wrath, selfish ambitions, dissensions, heresies, envy, murders, drunkenness, revelries, and the like, of which I tell you beforehand, just as I also told you in time past, that those who practice such things will not inherit the kingdom of God" (Galatians 5:19–21). While an evil spirit—the spirit of Murder, for instance—may tempt or compel someone to take another life, the actual deed is an act of the will.

Whatever their names, demons/evil spirits are clever beings. (All phrases in bold in the following Scripture verses are my emphasis.)

They are able to teach: "The Spirit clearly says that in later times, some will abandon the faith and follow deceiving spirits and things **taught by demons**" (1 Timothy 4:1 NIV).

They are powerful: "A man with an evil spirit came from the tombs to meet him. This man lived in the tomb, and **no one**

could bind him any more, not even with a chain" (Mark 5:2–3 NIV).

They are knowledgeable: "Moreover, demons came out of many people, shouting, '**You are the Son of God!**'" (Luke 4:41 NIV).

They believe: "You believe that there is one God. Good! Even the demons **believe** that—and shudder" (James 2:19 NIV).

They know the future: "'What do you want with us, Son of God?' they shouted. 'Have you come here to torture us **before the appointed time?**'" (Matthew 8:29 NIV).

They shout: "With **shrieks,** evil spirits came out of many, and many paralytics and cripples were healed" (Acts 8:7 NIV).

They have various levels of wickedness: "Then it goes and takes with it seven other spirits **more wicked than itself,** and they go in and live there" (Matthew 12:45 NIV).

They recognize authority: "Go away! What do you want with us, Jesus of Nazareth? Have you come to destroy us? I know who you are—**the Holy One of God!**" (Luke 4:34 NIV).

If, by now, you are a little discouraged with all this talk about demons and their apparent powers, just remember: "He who is in you [Jesus] is greater than he who is in the world [Satan and his minions]" (1 John 4:4).

Steps to Freedom

Green as we were, and knowing only a bit about the characteristics of evil spirits, we were entirely dependent upon Holy Spirit to guide us through each encounter. And He never disappointed. But we were careful to stay close to Him, following the biblical guidelines.

While people may feel overwhelmed by the demonic entities harassing them and may desperately want them gone, this very desperation will enable them to receive their deliverance. This may be instantaneous or a process. (We will use the personal pronoun *you* in listing the steps. If this applies to you, just know that you will never be able to help others until you yourself are set free.)

1. Confess. Be honest. If you are trapped in sin, confess it. "If we confess our sins, He is faithful and just to forgive us our sins and to cleanse us from all unrighteousness" (1 John 1:9). The devil and his demons cannot stand in the light of an honest confession.

2. Repent. Turn away from anything that may have opened the door to the evil spirit(s) and run to the Lord. Then, renounce all known sin and ask Holy Spirit to reveal anything hidden that is not of Him. "Repent, and let every one of you be baptized in the name of Jesus Christ for the remission of sins; and you shall receive the gift of the Holy Spirit" (Acts 2:38).

3. Ask God's forgiveness, then forgive anyone who has wronged or hurt you. This is absolutely crucial. Without forgiveness, you are likely to hang on to an offense that will cause a root of bitterness or resentment to spring up. This means the demonic spirit can take up residence in the fertile soil of your wounded heart. And be sure to forgive yourself too. "Forgive us our debts, as we forgive our debtors" (Matthew 6:12).

Remember the story of the unmerciful servant in Matthew 18? He was forgiven a large sum of money, as his master had compassion on him, yet he failed to forgive a small debt owed to him. God's warning to such a person is pretty severe—He will turn that person over to "the torturers": "So My heavenly Father will do to you if each of you, from his heart, does not forgive his brother his trespasses" (vv. 34–35).

And don't overlook verses 21–22: "Then Peter came to Him and said, 'Lord, how often shall my brother sin against me, and I forgive him? Up to seven times?' Jesus said to him, 'I do not say to you, up to seven times, but up to seventy times seven.'"

Forgive me, but I do need to emphasize once more the importance of forgiveness. Let me draw you a picture. When we withhold forgiveness from someone, our heavenly Father will turn us over to the "torturers," the tormentors, and the jailers. We create a prison cell for those we do not forgive—and for ourselves. They are on one side of the bars; we, on the other. It is cold and dark in there. Only the key of forgiveness will release both to emerge into the warmth and brilliance of the Sonlight. The proof of forgiveness is being able to remember the offense without pain or anger. This is real freedom.

4. Call on the name of the Lord. Forget caring what anyone around you may think and take the leap of faith that He will meet you, heal you, and set you free. "Call to Me, and I will answer you, and show you great and mighty things which you do not know" (Jeremiah 33:3).

5. Command the evil spirit(s) to leave—by name if you know them—using the authority God has given believers, along with His Word, which brings life. "In My name they will cast out demons" (Mark 16:17).

6. Declare your freedom to the principalities and powers of darkness, based on Jesus' finished work. "There is therefore now no condemnation to those who are in Christ Jesus who do not walk according to the flesh, but according to the Spirit. For the law of the Spirit of life in Christ has made me free from the law of sin and death" (Romans 8:1–2).

Here is a sample prayer of deliverance, or you may phrase your own. But it is important to pray out loud, declaring your confession and commitment.

Lord Jesus, I acknowledge You as my Savior and Lord. You are truly the Son of God. I thank You that Your blood has cleansed me, for You died for me, were buried, and rose from the dead on the third day. I am forgiven and seated with You in heavenly places. I forgive all those who have wronged me, and I forgive myself as You have forgiven me. (Take time for the Holy Spirit to show you whom to forgive.)

Again, Lord Jesus, I thank You for forgiving me. I thank You for the power of Your name and the power of Your blood. I renounce all works of the enemy in my life; I renounce all curses, all demonic influences. I break all yokes and snares. I command them all to loose me this very moment in the name of Jesus Christ! In the name of Jesus, I speak against all powers of the enemy and I command you to go from me right now, never to return!

Now, allow the power of the Holy Spirit to begin work in you, releasing anything that might come to mind. Forcefully breathe out several times. Look to Jesus, who is our Deliverer.

But don't stop there. To maintain your freedom:

- Be thankful continually; Satan cannot sow anything in a grateful heart. Put on "a garment of praise" (Isaiah 61:3).
- Make Jesus Lord over all of your life (see Matthew 22:37).
- Put on the full armor of God (see Ephesians 6).
- Live by and in God's Word, which is powerful for the "pulling down of strongholds" (2 Corinthians 10:4).
- Submit to God and resist the devil, and he will have to flee from you (see James 4:7).
- Join others in fellowship and walk in the light with them. Don't be a lone ranger (see Hebrews 10:25).

The bottom line of deliverance from demonic entities is simple: Just read the accounts of what Jesus did—and then imitate Him. In other words, say what He said and do what He did. Then watch what God will do.

Once you are free and have led others out of the darkness of the demonic into His marvelous light, don't forget to shut the door!

Chapter 11

Wounded Healer

He was wounded for our transgressions,
He was bruised for our iniquities;
The chastisement for our peace was upon Him,
And by His stripes we are healed.
Isaiah 53:5

As unbelievers when Doug and I were first married, the idea of supernatural healing in our day had honestly never occurred to us. That is, it had not occurred to us until we were confronted with the serious illness of our first child when he was only a year old.

Little Doug was simply not thriving. He suffered with constant diarrhea and was refusing any foods we attempted to introduce to him. At twelve months, he weighed only eighteen pounds, and we, along with the pediatrician we consulted, were stumped. In fact, our local doctor contacted a colleague from the University of Florida Medical School to discuss the case. Meanwhile, the poor little guy was only growing weaker.

Together, they arrived at a trial diet for him, consisting of overripe banana, cottage cheese, and round steak, scraped and browned. When he improved somewhat, the doctors concluded that he had celiac disease. Not curable, but manageable.

In the meantime, Doug's sister Bootsie, whom you met in an

earlier chapter, had been gloriously saved and filled with the Holy Spirit. Hearing about her little nephew's illness, Bootsie spread the word among all the intercessors in the state of Florida. We were impressed that people who didn't even know us were praying for our son.

When he was eighteen months, we noticed that little Doug's appetite had improved, and by the time he was two and a half, he was able to eat all the foods toddlers need with no ill effects. Even the pediatrician had to admit that this little one was apparently "cured." We were beginning to suspect that it was much more than that.

"Maybe It's Real!"

In 1971, the year Doug and I received Jesus as our Savior and experienced the baptism of the Holy Spirit, my younger sister Pam was diagnosed with lupus, an autoimmune disorder, complicated by nephritis, inflammation of the kidneys. Her condition was so serious that she was having to inject heparin into her abdomen daily. By now, I didn't put anything past the power of our risen Lord—even total healing.

Pam, on the other hand, needed some convincing. Having read a book by Kathryn Kuhlman on the subject of healing, I wrote my sister and sent her a copy, urging her to read it for herself. She read the book, noting that Kuhlman emphasized "the baptism of the Holy Spirit."

With renewed hope, Pam contacted an Episcopal priest with whom she had served on a national committee. When she mentioned the baptism of the Holy Spirit to him, he said, "Well, some people in my congregation tell me they have had that experience. Maybe it's real."

With his encouragement, Pam's next stop was to a prayer meeting held in a Catholic hospital where a nun, Sister Blige, prayed for her. It was then my sister heard the audible voice of the Lord, saying, "My healing power is in you. Go in peace."

As if that were not enough of God's goodness and mercy for one day, she was instructed to go home and lie down beside her husband, Tom. Tommy was a devout Catholic who loved God but had never been taught about His power available through the Holy Spirit. When Pam lay down beside Tommy, the fire of God hit that bed.

"I'm healed!" Pam cried out, feeling a rush of exhilaration. There was not a doubt in her mind. When you have a personal encounter with the living God, whatever you think you know bows the knee, and there is full assurance.

Two days later, Pam and Tommy made the trip from Tampa to a research hospital in Gainesville to consult with her doctor, who seemed baffled by her seeming turnaround. He suggested, "Let's rerun the tests."

When the second set of tests confirmed that the disease was, indeed, no longer evident, he admitted that she was free of lupus. Jubilant over this good news, on the way home from Gainesville in their red convertible, Tommy began praying in tongues— something unheard of in his church.

Fired up by this incredible experience, he decided to study the Scriptures for himself. He attended a Baptist school, leaving the Catholic Church for that season. Upon graduation, he was persuaded by his former priest to return to the church as a lay evangelist. For the past fifty years, Tommy has traveled the world, preaching the gospel of Jesus Christ in China, Eastern Europe, Africa, and throughout the United States—the fruit of one woman's healing.

Pam lived, disease-free, for twenty years before needing a kidney transplant. Not long after that, she moved to heaven, but not before founding a school of prayer to raise up the next generation of intercessors. God gave my sister additional years to serve Him and bless others, and radically touched my brother-in-law, who picked up the torch and continues the good work to this day.

It's My Turn

It is one thing to testify to another person's supernatural healing. It's quite another when it happens to *you*. I literally "stumbled" into what would become a powerful part of my testimony and, ultimately, a vital part of ministry.

One Saturday evening when leaving a friend's house after dinner, I was walking down the sidewalk when I turned my ankle and heard a loud crack. There was no question I had a broken bone.

Doug wanted to take me to Vandy, as the world-famous hospital was not far from our friend's home, but I didn't want to go. Instead, I hobbled to the car and when we reached our house, I hopped inside and crawled to our bedroom, then hoisted myself onto the bed.

When Doug kept insisting I ought to see a doctor, I was adamant. "No, I want *God* to heal me." If He could do that for my son and my sister, I knew He could do it for me.

The next morning, Sunday, I was determined to go to church. My ankle couldn't hurt any worse there than it was hurting at home. When Doug saw that I was getting dressed, he gave me a hand. Holding onto his arm, I slowly made my way down the hall toward the front door. All the way, he was proclaiming Scripture over me: "By His stripes, you are healed. . . . He sent His Word and healed you. . . . In Jesus' name, be healed."

My ankle was healed before we got to church!

Nobody will believe this, but by Tuesday morning I was playing tennis. With no X-ray to prove it, I *absolutely knew* I was healed. But there was one regret. All this was so new to me that I failed to give my testimony about this miraculous occurrence. In His mercy, God had another surprise in store for me.

———

A few years later, I was on my way to worship in Scott and Sarah MacLeod's big tent, having just come from interceding for the nation at a gathering in downtown Nashville. Walking across the grass to the tent, I broke both ankles! Don't ask me how I managed to do that, although I strongly suspected that, as an intercessor, I had entered a spiritual minefield and had been wounded in action. This time, there was such stabbing pain it would be impossible to maneuver myself to the tent or the car.

Fortunately, two EMTs who had come to worship quickly rushed to my side and helped me into Kim Driver's car for a trip to the ER at a hospital in Franklin. By then, both ankles were extremely swollen and painful and were beginning to turn black. After several X-rays, the doctor on call put my ankles in casts. This time, there would be no hobbling, hopping, or crawling. I was immobilized in my plaster prison.

Hospitalized overnight, in pain, feverish and chilling, I turned my thoughts to those Chinese pastors, many of whom were even now being imprisoned in a cold cell for their faith in Jesus—with no blanket to keep them warm. As I prayed for them, wrapped in my own heated blanket, suddenly the Presence of the Lord filled my room. It was so powerful yet so soothing and sweet that I felt no more pain.

Released from the hospital the next morning, I was still astonishingly pain-free, and in only nine days, it was as if nothing had ever happened.

Before being discharged, I had been ordered to return for additional X-rays as a precautionary follow-up. Although I did return as requested—every month for a while—there was never any further problem. No pins in my ankles. No surgery necessary.

By February, when I had my monthly X-ray, the technician was astounded. "You are growing calcium in your ankle bones. That's not supposed to be there!"

You know the rest of the story. The Lord was doing what He does best—healing and restoring. In fact, He had told me earlier, *I've got this. I saw what happened . . . and I didn't like it one bit!*

There was no question that I would gladly testify to His goodness, His grace, and His healing power this time, also being careful to include the *first* time He had supernaturally healed me.

Hip, Hip, Hurray?

Don't know what it is about my bones, but not long ago, I had to have a hip replacement. I was now in my seventies, and this was no small procedure. As a matter of fact, during the surgery, my blood pressure dropped so low, the anesthetist had to pull the anesthesia. As you may know, with hip replacements, a saw is used, so the pain was horrific. Not only that, but I could sense the anxiety in the medical team hovering over me as I lay on the operating table. It was not a scenario that I would ever want to relive.

Just take me home right now, Lord! I begged silently. *This is unbearable! I mean it! Take me home!*

I recalled another conversation I'd had with Him earlier when considering the price many Chinese Christians and others have to pay for their faith. I had asked, "Will there be enough of You in me to endure when they pull off my fingernails, Lord? Or will I deny You?"

It was my fervent hope and prayer that I would never deny Him. Yet, I wanted this pain to stop. And once again, His dear Presence flooded the room and my heart, and I knew only pure joy—so much so that when a nurse came to check on me after the surgery, she inspected the IV line to see what medication they were giving me. But it was His love that was taking care of my pain.

This supernatural peace and joy lasted eight days.

I was home by the ninth day, when the joy lifted. While a physical therapist was working with me one afternoon, I slammed my cane down on my toe and broke it. That night, I fell out of bed onto the side where my new hip was still healing. *Lord, what is happening to me?*

I tried my best to process these unfortunate "accidents"—or

were they demonic attacks . . . or something else? Sobbing, I called a friend, Shannon McLaird, and asked her, "Is this trauma on me—or the land?"

"It could be both," Shannon replied.

After finding spent bullets in our yard, which Civil War buffs could identify as either from the North or South, Doug and I figured that our property had been the site of some battle during the Civil War, with brother killing brother. This had likely brought a curse. Several days later, Shannon and Carol Goodwin came to pray over me and the land.

A couple of weeks passed before I was able to walk without assistance. Following the Holy Spirit's lead, Doug and I stepped out onto our lawn, confessed and repented of the sins of our forefathers, forgave the embattled troops on our property, then took communion, pouring the leftover wine over the land.

Feeling the chill since it was late February, we hurried back inside as fast as I could manage. Through the kitchen window, I could see an apple tree, gnarled and withered in the icy grip of winter, and remembered a Scripture that applied to the land, to the tree, and to me: "I shall not die, but live!" (Psalm 118:17). I declared those words prophetically—over the land, over the tree, and over me—and felt the curse lift.

By spring, the apple tree blossomed, and in due time, it bore fruit, its heavy branches dragging the ground. There were so many apples, we had to call in help for the harvest. I long to be that fruitful in my life and ministry—requiring help for the harvest.

The Great Physician—and His Helping Hands

Sometimes God, the ultimate Healer, uses doctors and hospitals to assist in healing. I had a spinal condition that suddenly worsened. My legs would give way and I would do a face plant. If the Lord didn't heal me supernaturally, I was headed for a wheelchair, so I felt led to get some human help. Contacting a surgical nurse friend, I asked her advice as to the best neurosurgeon in the area.

"I'll pray about it," she assured me, then got back with me in the next few days. "Dr. Oren Aaronson is head of Neurosurgery, now associated with a fine hospital in town. He's the surgeon to consult in case that is the recommended course."

I called his office and made an appointment. It was already intriguing to me that his name, "Aaronson," means "son of Aaron," the brother of Moses. I was even more impressed when we met him. Although British, the doctor had grown up in Israel, but had lived in the States since his residency.

"So, I suppose you served in the IDF while in Israel, right?" I knew that service in the Israeli Defense Force is compulsory for all citizens—male and female—for two years, beginning at the age of eighteen.

He nodded. "Yes, I did."

"Then you're tough, aren't you?"

He smiled and his one-word answer told me everything I needed to know. "Yes."

From that moment on, I felt an immediate kinship with this surgeon and peace, or *shalom*, in Hebrew, filled my soul.

As we discussed my symptoms, the doctor was reassuring. "I think I can help you, but your problem will require four procedures."

I had never heard of a "good" back surgery, and here he was suggesting a quite complicated one. But I had no doubt that the Holy Spirit had led me to Dr. Aaronson, and we scheduled the surgery.

When I woke up from the anesthesia, Dr. Aaronson was standing beside me. Looking down, he said with great satisfaction, "It was just beautiful."

True to his word, it *was* beautiful. By fusing two vertebrae, reconstructing two more, and completing two additional procedures, I now have 70 percent more room in my spine. Within eight months, I was walking five miles a day. In London later that year, there was a twelve-hour layover before boarding a flight to Israel. During that layover, our group—and I—walked all over the city. No back pain!

Right before Our Eyes

Fresh from the Pensacola outpouring mentioned earlier, an Episcopal priest in Nashville was filled with the fire of God. Hearing about his anointed messages, Doug and I attended a service.

Sitting in the pew in front of us was an elderly gentleman. Midway through the sermon, he turned around and whispered loudly, "I think I've been healed of Parkinson's disease. What should I do?"

Doug leaned forward to answer him. "Go up and tell the father that you've been healed."

The gentleman made his way to the front and stood before the pulpit. The priest paused in his sermon and asked graciously, "How can I help you, sir?"

"Just wanted to tell you that I've been healed of Parkinson's disease."

"Oh, really? And how do you know?"

"Well, if you had Parkinson's and stopped shaking, you'd know you had been healed too."

I couldn't help thinking that, during His earthly ministry, Jesus was interrupted all the time—to answer questions, to create wine from water and multiply bread and fish, to heal. What made this even more amazing was the fact that by interrupting the proceedings, the entire congregation heard the man's testimony of God's healing—right before their eyes.

Wounded Healer

The One who bore all our sins and sicknesses in His own perfect body on the cross knows how to sympathize with our pain. And those of us who have suffered in some way physically perhaps have greater understanding and compassion for those who are sick.

In any case, whether I see healing manifested or not, I never want to pass up an opportunity to pray for the sick. Our Lord can be trusted with every prayer, and I bow to His will. As He says in Jeremiah 1:12, "I am watching over My word to perform it" (TLV).

Chapter 12

Just Say Yes!

*We're not called to live by human reason. All that matters
is obedience to God's Word and His leading in our lives.
If He says go, we'll go. If He says stay, we'll stay. When we are
in His will, we are in the safest place in the world.*
Brother Yun, *The Heavenly Man*

Perhaps the most important word I could deliver in this season of my life is something I have been sharing everywhere I go recently. The question I have been led to ask myself—and now you—is this: "Where am I spending myself? Is it for some cause—or for Christ alone?" This question is a plumbline dropped into the middle of our lives to check our status with the Lord. And, now as never before, it is imperative that we know the answer.

Several months ago, a Jewish believer named Michael N. and his wife flew in from Israel to attend a family wedding. When time came for them to make the return trip, they heard that war had broken out in their homeland, and they were forced to remain in the States for an extended period.

Tod McDowell suggested that we host an impromptu meeting at the Caleb ranch house and ask Michael to update us on what was going on in Israel. We met on a Tuesday evening, and without having announced the gathering in church, the place was packed. People were literally sitting on the stairs—all the way to the top.

In Jerusalem, Michael had been given an office at Christ Church, the oldest Protestant church building in the Middle East, because of his common vision of the founders of Christ Church—to preach the gospel from Jerusalem to the rest of the Middle East. That year, he was asked to preach the Good Friday message to a group of Christian tourists.

"As a good Jewish boy, I had never celebrated Good Friday—even after I became a believer. Really knew very little about it," he confessed. "So, you can imagine that I had some cramming to do before that message."

Michael studied the Gospel of John and, to his surprise, realized that 40 percent of the book deals with the last week of Jesus' life on earth. That fact alone rocked him.

"When I began reading, I had to wonder if John the Beloved, as he was called, would make it to the very end with Jesus." Under his breath, Michael added, "Of course, the *women* did."

At this comment, there were a few appreciative chuckles from the audience.

"Peter made it into the courtyard. But when Jesus was being tried before Pilate, Peter wasn't around. Because of John's relationship with Jesus, John went into the court with Him.

"You see, Peter was interested in the cause—the coming kingdom—and when he saw it wasn't going to happen anytime soon, he said, 'I'm going fishing.' But John made it all the way to the cross." Michael paused before making a stunning statement that has resonated with me ever since: "A *cause* will never take you where you *want* to go. Only the *cross* will take you where you *need* to go."

There are so many worthwhile causes out there—good causes. For example, I'm very passionate about race relations. I'm passionate about opposing abortion. These causes seem so noble—and they are. Yet, we can be so close and still miss the reason we're here. Jesus Himself said, "The poor you will always have with you" (Matthew 26:11 NIV). But we must listen for His voice speaking precisely and personally to each one of us, keep our gaze fixed on Him, and not become sidetracked from our destiny.

Finding Our Purpose

I hate to admit that I was sixty years old before I discovered my real purpose. Things were about as clear as a stained-glass window. Still, I should have picked up on some clues.

My first clue popped up when I was about nine and in the fourth grade. I noticed that my teacher did not have a watch, and watches were important as there were no wall clocks in classrooms back then. So I decided I would have to buy her one. Since my dad was Navy, I knew there was a PX on the base, and he could get a good watch for a really good price. I raised the money from classmates, and he was able to buy a gold watch for $75. The joy was not in giving the gift, but that my teacher received something she definitely needed. Although I knew nothing of the Bible at the time, I was learning that "it is more blessed to give than to receive" (Acts 20:35).

An incident the following year should have tipped me off as to the nature of my calling. On our way from Bartow, Florida, to Newport, Rhode Island, where my dad was stationed, Mother was driving us children (I was the oldest of four). In Virginia, we stopped at the family home. It was a typical Southern plantation with lots of acreage and several small huts that had served as slave quarters.

"I'm glad we lost that war," I muttered under my breath, thinking of the infamous Civil War that had been fought on this very ground.

"What makes you say a thing like that?" my mother huffed.

"Because we were wrong, and we *should* have lost!"

Looking back, I can see that this was only one of the issues on which my mother and I disagreed. In fact, I never really knew if she loved me—not until just before her death.

But it was an episode that took place a little later that should have given me the final hint as to my future. In Newport, we rented a big house. The landlady lived in a garage apartment behind the house. One stormy night, she stopped by to tell us that this was her last day to raise money for the annual March of Dimes drive and to ask Mom if she would let me ride around the neighborhood with her to knock on doors and collect funds.

After that conversation, two things came to mind:

1. My mother would never let me do that (yet she did), and . . .
2. I was made for this—daring adventure with a hint of danger. Standing on porches, knocking on doors in the pouring rain, with lightning crackling all around me, was a thrill. I loved it!

Look for the clues in your life—God plants them there. And, for Pete's sake, don't wait until you are sixty years old to let them lead you to the treasure of God's purpose for you. Then, don't forget to say yes.

Ridiculous . . . or Sublime?

Sometimes, when the Lord speaks, you may not be sure you have heard correctly. The marching order may sound outrageous. Take something I was led to do at the turn of this century, for example: *I want you to take the mark of this generation. Get a tattoo.*

Now, as the daughter of a Navy man, the only tattooed people I knew about were drunken sailors. But then came the year 2000, when so many young people were getting tattoos. Even the kids in church were getting them, and from somewhere deep within, I heard, *If you reject this generation, you have to reject Me.*

I remembered what Derek Prince had said: "Historically speaking, only 10 percent of the people of God who are touched in one move of God will say yes to God in the next move." Most people don't like change, only the radical ones. I wanted to be one of the radical ones.

I was walking through the house on the way to the laundry room with a basket of dirty clothes when I heard the Lord say something else: *Strap your sword on your thigh.*

Whaat?! I was supposed to get a tattoo . . . on my thigh?

Surely Doug would think it was a crazy idea, so I decided to ask him, "Could it be God?"

Oddly enough, he agreed. "Yes, I think it is."

Well, maybe I could get a tattoo that matched the varicose veins in my leg. But I was still hesitant.

Some of my friends tried to talk me out of it. "Dabney, do NOT do this!"

I had said yes to the Lord, but I was not marked yet. Maybe there was still a way out. About that time, Cindy Jacobs, the prophetic general, came to Belmont. In her message, she cautioned us not to reject kids with tattoos. To my chagrin, several people who knew of my struggle stood to their feet, chanting, "Go for it, Dabney! Go for it!"

On a trip to Scotland once, I had bought a miniature sword as a memento of my ancestor, the Black Douglas. Now I knew what to do with it. Still, I had no idea where a tattoo artist might hang out.

At church one day, I spotted one of the tattooed young people and asked, "Josh, where is the best place to get a tattoo in Nashville?"

His suggestion was a little studio, the Lone Wolf, across from Vanderbilt University.

Now that I was committed, I'd do it, but I would take a couple of intercessor friends with me to check out the shop and make an appointment. Located up some creaky stairs over a Chinese restaurant, that tattoo parlor was the darkest, most dismal place I had ever seen.

After meeting the young man who would do the deed, I showed him the little sword and told him what I wanted. He made a copy of the image, expecting me to have the procedure done right then and there.

"Oh, I'm sorry," I said. "I'm having gallbladder surgery next week, but I could come back the following week."

He gave me a curious look—as if he didn't really expect to see this middle-aged woman again. But I showed up at the appointed time, minus my gallbladder.

While sitting in his chair and before he proceeded to use that wicked-looking instrument on the outer part of my leg just above my knee, I asked, "Actually, I'm terrified right now. Do you mind if I run out to my car and get a CD to play while you're working on me?"

He shrugged. "Cool."

For the next forty-five minutes, while the girls were praying, that young man heard worship and intercession in the upbeat style of the "Elijah Revolution," featuring Lou Engle and Stacey Campbell as they prophesied, backed by a worship band. My tattoo artist loved it and played it on every loudspeaker in the place.

When he finished, I fished out the $100 fee from my purse, but he waved it away. "I don't want all that money." I knew then that the Lord had touched him.

"Oh, no, I want to pay you," I insisted. "As much as I dreaded having this done, you didn't hurt me at all. Thank you so much."

Don't know what happened with my young friend, but I do know that saying yes to the Holy Spirit's prompting has opened the door to many opportunities to witness to that generation.

For example, there was a time a couple of us from the School of Supernatural Living (SOSL) went out to find someone with whom to share God's love. Each week, we were instructed to ask the Lord to tell us four things about a person we would meet in ministry. I can recall only the first item on that list: the name Lily.

"Really, Lord?" I mumbled in disbelief. "People today don't name their children Lily these days. That's so old-fashioned."

My witnessing partner and I decided to look for our "person" in a local high-end grocery store. But we walked the aisles and, with the exception of one forlorn-looking boy, who didn't seem interested in making conversation, we turned up nothing. We kept walking, finally making our way to the plant section. *We're never going to find anyone,* I thought, discouraged.

When we reached a section with *peace* lilies for sale, I said to my friend, "You know, that generation is mine. I'm going back to talk to that young man."

He was still standing where we had first seen him, so I launched into my spiel. "I see you've got tattoos. So do I. I really like your tats. Let me see. Tell me about this one."

Suddenly, his countenance changed. "That one's for Lily." Not surprisingly, we had instant rapport.

When well-meaning Christians try to disagree with me on this subject, I console myself with the biblical truth that Jesus has my name tattooed on the palm of His hand.

My decision was further confirmed when I learned that when another SOSL student, Neal, went on a mission trip to Romania, the kids listened when he talked to them about the Lord—because of his tattoos. While he was speaking, several healings—including a horrible toothache—"just happened." Those young people didn't want anything to do with Jesus at first, but they could relate to Neal's tattoos.

So, whenever the Spirit suggests something absurd to you, just say yes. The ridiculous may lead to something utterly sublime.

First Things First

I sense that we are riding the crest of a wave right now, but I'm not sure what to do because I don't want to mess things up. Remember Uzzah in the Bible? He was the Israelite who tried to help God out by stabilizing the cart carrying the Ark of the Covenant when God had expressly forbidden anyone to touch it. The consequences were severe—death. God doesn't need our help.

This is a time to be very careful to hear His voice and follow His instructions to the letter. For example, there was a season when He was urging me to put everything aside and simply rest in Him. He was saying, *You've really been busy doing My work,* and He began to list my recent activities. *Now all I want from you is to be still.*

"But, Lord," I argued, "I need to go get my notepad at least." *You don't need a notepad. Just be still.*

"But I won't remember what You tell me." *You'll remember.*

After spending an hour in the room where I meet with the Lord, I came out, remembering everything I was supposed to remember. I felt so happy and free! Try it.

Listening and obeying are paramount for this next season. We are on the cusp of what we've been praying for, believing for. But God's methods may be packaged differently from anything we've been accustomed to. Be prepared for the extraordinary from our extraordinary God.

———

Recently, I heard of an incident that took place in an out-of-the-box church that operates in the prophetic. Each Sunday, people from all over the country come to experience the glory and anointing of God.

One Sunday, a man had a heart attack and collapsed during the worship service. A cardiac nurse, who was also in the audience, rushed over to administer CPR. But the Lord stopped her: *Don't touch him. I'm giving him a new heart.* Nevertheless, many gathered around him to pray for healing and to cast out any spirit of infirmity.

When the paramedics arrived a few minutes later, they declared the man dead. However, just as the medics were preparing to move the body to a gurney to be transported to the hospital morgue, the man sat up!

"Sir, maybe you ought to be checked out at the ER," one of the medics suggested.

"Nah," he said. "I want to finish my worship."

Things are happening! People are being healed in "ordinary" church services. The body of Christ is waking up from its long slumber.

Here I Am . . .

So, here I am . . . entering my eightieth year. I had always thought I would dread the idea of growing older, but it's really great. I'm having the time of my life, and I couldn't be happier with every day that dawns.

This may sound strange to you, but I have never felt the call of God on my life, but I have had a call on Him. I have begged Him to let me go, to minister, to love, to pray, to seek and to save those who are lost, to touch the untouched. This continues to be my desire for the remainder of my time on earth.

Adam and Eve were called to multiply the grace and glory of God, but they missed the mark. Today, like the first couple, even some of the people of God have sown division and separation from Him. I am asking Him to let me be one who helps to mend the tears in the fabric of my church, my city, my nation, and the world.

As you know, the world is changing. The pandemic has forced some countries to close and, thus, some opportunities for us to go.

But we don't have to wait until they reopen, for God has brought the nations to our doorstep. In our city, a true city of refuge, we now have a population that encompasses more than 140 language groups. I can love and serve right where I am. You can too.

One last request: Please don't let my book simply be another story slipped into your spiritual library. Listen for the personal challenge God is offering *you*.

But before I go, will you pray with me?

Father God, the years are rolling by, and You know the plans You have for me—for each of us. Keep us supple in Your hands, particularly in these tumultuous times. Filter everything we see and hear through the knowledge of You with ever-increasing hope and faith. Pour Yourself out into all the nations—a rainbow of color and cultures.

Above all, Lord, bless the company of women who labor in Your vineyard, often unseen and unnoticed. Raise them up to be Deborahs, Esthers, Hannahs, and Ruths. Transform the Rahabs into Rachels, the Jezebels into jewels in Your crown. You see them. You love them. You know their names.

And, if You would be so kind, Lord, in every way that I am able, may I continue to impart My passion for You and Your kingdom to the next generation—until You come. May we be fully equipped and ready, filled with Your fire, when You say, "Go!"

ENDNOTES

1 "Creation of Israel, 1948," Office of the Historian, https://history.state.gov/milestones/1945-1952/creation-israel.

2 Pat Alexander, "Hijacked Hostages Rescue a Miracle, Sister Says," *The Tennessean*, July 5, 1976, 11.

3 Ibid.

4 "Smith Wigglesworth," Wikipedia, https://en.wikipedia.org/wiki/Smith_Wigglesworth.

5 https://billygraham.org/story/awakening-a-sleeping-giant-in-south-dakota/.

6 Much of the material in this chapter is taken from Doug's notes, copied during sessions conducted by Derek Prince.

7 See Agnes Sanford's book, *The Healing Gifts of the Spirit*, for help with inner healing. She has written other books, and I have read everything I could find by this author. In addition, we have found the SOZO model from Bethel Church, Redding, California, to give much direction for inner healing, as well as Theo Therapy.

Made in the USA
Monee, IL
20 April 2023